GUNN'S GOLDEN RULES

GUNN'S GOLDEN RULES

Life's Little Lessons for Making It Work

TIM GUNN

with Ada Calhoun

G

GALLERY BOOKS

New York   London   Toronto   Sydney

G𝕋

Gallery Books
A Division of Simon & Schuster, Inc.
1230 Avenue of the Americas
New York, NY 10020

First Gallery Books hardcover edition September 2010

GALLERY BOOKS and colophon are trademarks of Simon & Schuster, Inc.

For information about special discounts for bulk purchases,
please contact Simon & Schuster Special Sales at 1-866-506-1949
or business@simonandschuster.com.

The Simon & Schuster Speakers Bureau can bring authors to your
live event. For more information or to book an event contact the
Simon & Schuster Speakers Bureau at 1-866-248-3049 or visit our website
at www.simonspeakers.com.

Designed by Joy O'Meara

Manufactured in the United States of America

5 7 9 10 8 6 4

Library of Congress Cataloging-in-Publication Data
Gunn, Tim.
Gunn's golden rules : life's little lessons for making it work / by Tim Gunn,
with Ada Calhoun.
p.   cm.
1. Gunn, Tim. Project runway (Television program). 2. Clothing and
dress—United States. 3. Life skills—United States. I. Calhoun, Ada.
II. Title.
TT507 .G858 2010   746.9'2092—dc22
2010012417

ISBN 978-1-4391-7656-6
ISBN 978-1-4391-7767-9 (ebook)

❦{ CONTENTS }❧

CONTENTS

GUNN'S GOLDEN RULES

O N *Project Runway,* I enter the workroom and offer my thoughts—as a mentor, not a judge—on the designers' work. The advice I give most often is to "make it work."

That's not just a catchphrase. It's a philosophy I've followed my whole life, and I credit it with all the wonderful and surprising success I've had as a TV personality, teacher, and writer. What "make it work" means is that you should use what you have on hand to transform your situation. It's always possible to use whatever tools you have at your disposal to create something that you're proud of and that gets the job done.

Far too often in classes I've taught I've seen students throw out a lot of hard work and start again from scratch. They may wind up with a good garment, but they aren't learning the skills that are essential to excelling in a creative field: patience, innovation, and diligence.

I love to see students trying to learn as they go along. The designers and artists I admire spend their whole lives learning. Everything they make may not be a commercial success, but every bit of effort they make gets them closer to realizing their vision.

One of the things I admire about *Project Runway* is that it's really about developing creative design work. I'll never forget a woman coming up to me at an airport and saying that she loved *Runway* because she felt it set such a good example for her nine-year-old daughter. "It demonstrates that good qualities of character—like hard work and persistence—pay off, and cheaters never prosper," she said.

Well, that was one of the nicest things anyone's ever said to me. I love to think that we're setting a good example in that way.

Few people remember it now, but *Project Runway* was quite controversial in the beginning. It took the mystique out of the fashion world and said, "This is a demanding, gut-wrenching industry. You need a really strong drive and love for the work in order to be successful."

I guess we shouldn't have been shocked, but people in this industry did not react well. They thought we were taking the glamour out of fashion. The design world had been enshrouded in a kind of veil of mystery, and *Project Runway* pulled it back to let the world see it for what it was, warts and all. We got some very nasty reviews and some very harsh comments from our colleagues.

But we wanted to tell the truth. And the truth is that in this business, crazy crises happen, like when you're waiting for the knits to get off the boat from China and the show is tomorrow and the boat doesn't dock. What do you do? Remove fourteen looks from the show? You make it work, somehow. It's a fashion 911, and you have to respond to it. You can't pretend it doesn't exist.

Now the industry has bought in to the show's concept completely, and everyone pretends they loved *Project Runway* all along. Well, I'm happy that the show's become so popular and that everyone is so full of praise for it, but I do remember those early days, when we were treated as though we were magicians telling everyone how the rabbit got in the hat.

I like to think that my role in the fashion industry has been a bit like *Project Runway*'s position among reality shows, which is a voice of simple reason. Let others be shimmery and flashy and brilliant. (And no one loves daring geniuses more than I do.) I will always be there in the wings saying, "You need to be good to people. You need to take your work seriously. You need to have integrity. You need to work with what you've got."

A woman behind me in line at Starbucks the other day introduced herself as an assistant at a popular women's magazine.

"Are you taking a break?" I asked.

"No, I'm here getting coffee for everyone." She laughed a bitter laugh and showed me a mile-long list.

"It's all in the details," I said. "Do everything one thousand percent. You could be editor in chief some day!"

I'm afraid she thought I was teasing her, but the fact is I am constitutionally incapable of being snarky. I'm not throwing out barbs and making fun of people. I believe in giving a dimension of seriousness to the whole enterprise of creating and talking about clothes, even to red-carpet reportage, and I'm very proud of that.

As anyone who's been on the red carpet can tell you, the experience is *terrifying*. You're always just a hair shy of enduring a humiliating moment or facing someone who's just there to make fun of you. I thought: *I need to be an antidote to all this horrible stuff.*

As many people who watch *Project Runway* know, I am a stickler for good manners, and I believe that treating other people well is a lost art. In the workplace, at the dinner table, and walking down the street—we are confronted with choices on how to treat people nearly every waking moment. Over time these choices define who we are and whether we have a lot of friends and allies or none.

So how do we do this social thing well? And by "well," I mean: How do we become more respectful and further our own goals at the same time? Dear reader, these two concepts are not mutually exclusive; they're mutually beneficial—and that's what this book is all about.

To maintain anything like a good working relationship with people, to get by in the world successfully, you need to have good manners. (And you need a sense of humor or you may as well slit your wrists.)

I reflect on manners, or the lack of them, each and every day. There are times when I want to stop the world for a moment and ask certain people some probing questions, such as: All of these people are trying to get off the subway train. Why do you six people think you should enter before we leave? Don't you realize that if you just clear a path we can get off and you can get on?

In the Internet age, even the very word *manners* seems antiquated.

Life moves so rapidly these days that it's easy to feel justified in being rude.

"I'm rushing home to the babysitter. That's why I didn't say 'thank you' to the cashier."

"If I treat my assistant humanely, maybe it will be taken as a sign of weakness and I will lose my job."

"I get so many e-mails, there's no time to respond, much less to be eloquent."

With the advent of certain omnipresent technological devices, with chivalry long gone, with message boards teaching young people that anonymous rudeness is acceptable, we are looking at a great amount of change for the worse.

But let us not be swept up in this tide of rudeness. This book (in addition to being a fun excuse to tell some of my favorite fashion-world stories) is a call to arms, a manifesto for kindness, generosity, and integrity. I hope you will join me in trying to make society a friendlier, more polite, and less aggressive place.

Of course, it's not like I am perfect. I've made many mistakes, and I continue to slip up now and then in my effort to behave well. And you'll hear all about it!

And yet I always atone for my errors, and there are certain fundamental social protocols I've come to hold dear: I don't believe in texting while dining, sending one-word e-mails in lieu of formal thank-you cards, wearing shorts to the theater, or settling for any of the modern trends that favor comfort over politeness, ease over style.

Being a good friend to other people, being glamorous and attractive, being a success are no accidents. Having a rich career and home life are the result of a great deal of hard work.

But that doesn't mean the work isn't fun.

In this book, I will share my thoughts on what constitutes a life well lived. These rules are what I've always tried to impart to my students and have tried to follow in my own career and social life. In writing these chapters, I've tried to think of you, the readers, as beloved students who have come to me during office hours to ask advice, talk over a dilemma, or just hang out.

Good manners lead to better relationships, more career success, and less personal stress. Manners are a relief, not a terrible obligation. It's my belief that etiquette isn't cold and formal; it's warm and flexible. I am very concerned with manners, but I am not a robot. Manners are simply about asking yourself, What's the right thing to do?

I deeply believe that if we all have this simple question in our minds, we will do right by one another. We won't always succeed . . . As you will learn from this book, in the course of trying to do the right thing, I have let a closet full of unopened gifts pile up in my apartment, overextended myself to the point where I almost had a nervous breakdown, and even put a dear old lady in the hospital!

But I've learned from every mistake, and I'm eager for you to learn from them, too. In that spirit, I will be offering my thoughts on manners, reminiscing about my own experiences adhering or failing to measure up to them, and telling what I hope are entertaining stories—not *too* many scandalous ones, but I do have a few doozies . . .

So please, pull up a chair and let's start our chat!

Make It Work!

A S A LITTLE KID, when confronted with a difficult situation, I would run and hide somewhere in our Washington, D.C., house. I wanted to escape from the world. School, sports, church, birthday parties—anything social terrified me. All I wanted to do was hole up until the event had passed and I could go back to reading alone in my room.

Unfortunately, I couldn't stay hidden for very long, because the house wasn't that big and eventually my mother figured out my favorite hiding places. But usually it would be long enough to scare the living daylights out of her, which for me was not an unhappy side effect.

As my mother caught on to each new scheme, I got more creative. I think it was maybe the third or fourth time I hid, I actually ran away outside and found a good secluded spot in the yard. I was thrilled when I heard her inside tearing the house apart. Finally, I had really succeeded in terrorizing her. I could have stayed out in that yard forever.

Well, unfortunately for my escapist fantasies, we had a basset hound, Brandy. My mother sent Brandy out to find me, and she did so immediately.

This made me more determined. I thought: *I need to get smarter about this. I need to run away* with *Brandy.*

That didn't work, either, because my parents would yell for me and Brandy would bark back.

Then it became a challenge to run away with her *and* to keep my hand over her mouth.

The whole project got more and more complicated until, ultimately, I decided it was less trouble just to stay home and be miserable.

In that moment, the seeds of "make it work!" were born. Running away from my problems didn't help. I had to face up to whatever it was that I didn't want to deal with—my homework, an angry parent, a fight with a friend—rather than just trying to put it off until it went away. Until you address them, I have since learned, such problems never truly vanish.

I had to make the best of the bad situation. What I found was that if I did that, the situation would rapidly become less bad, whereas if I hid from it or tried to make it go away, I would get more and more anxious and the situation would get worse and worse. I learned very early the wisdom of making it—whatever *it* was—work.

The phrase "make it work!" came later, but it didn't originate on *Project Runway*. I began using it in my classroom when I was a design teacher at Parsons, the celebrated design college in Manhattan where I worked for twenty-four years. I found it to be an extremely useful mantra when my students were in trouble.

One such example came during a later phase of my academic career. I was teaching Concept Development to seniors.

This was a six-hour class that met once a week for the entire academic year—two fifteen-week semesters. It was a long time to work on a single project, and students learned a lot by having to go deep into their own unique concepts.

The year began with the crystallization of each student's thesis: five to seven head-to-toe looks that represented their point of view as a designer. (It was Joan Kaner, the celebrated style maven and former vice president of Neiman Marcus, who once said to me, "I can tell everything that I need to know about a designer from five looks." I think about that all the time.)

Those looks were executed in muslin (an unbleached cotton fabric used for prototyping) in a corresponding course that was appropriately called Studio Methods. I would visit that class on a regular basis, especially during fittings, which happened every two weeks.

On the topic of fittings, I forbade my students from designing for themselves or using themselves as fit models for their collection. Why? Because when you wear your own designs, you lose objectivity. It's important that each designer maintain a well-honed ability to critically analyze his or her own work. If you're only ever designing for your own body, you'd better be prepared to have a clientele of one.

I like the *Project Runway* Season 7 designer Ping Wu, who famously used herself as a mannequin, as a person even though she's exhausting to be around. She has so much personality. When I told her at the end of Episode 3, "The workroom won't be the same without you," I meant it! I had to talk Jesse LeNoir off a ledge during their team challenge. He's a lovely guy and quite talented. He recognized many of the problems the judges saw, but he couldn't convince Ping to fix them.

When we had the auditions, I found her work compelling but her pieces were all hand knits. I said, "How do you translate this to *Project Runway*? Would you do sewn knits? They won't have the same Möbius-strip quality."

In some ways I think she was handicapped by being a hand-knit designer, and by using herself as a dress form. As you may remember, in Episode 2, the model's rear end was hanging out of her skirt. It was vulgar. Ping's practice of using herself as a model clouded her objectivity. I think that's a big part of why she made it only to Episode 3.

One instance in which "make it work!" came in particularly handy was during the spring semester of 2002. One of my students, Emma, was seriously struggling with the silhouette and proportions of the items that made up the looks in her collection. We had three fit models before us, and frankly, the collection was a hot mess.

I was struggling, too, in my efforts to get Emma to see solutions. What exactly was it that was so wrong? Even I couldn't describe it. The only word that came to mind was *everything*. She was frustrated to the point of tears when she declared that she was going to throw everything away and begin again from scratch.

"You are not starting over," I responded. "Besides, even if I agreed that you should, you've put twenty-five weeks into this collection, and it will be presented to the thesis jury in a month. It will be impossible to present anything of quality in that short amount of time." (This was before *Project Runway*, which would recalibrate my thinking about time!)

"Then what am I going to do?" Emma asked, looking at me helplessly.

"You don't have time to reconceive your designs, to shop for new fabric, or to make new muslins," I replied. "You're going to diagnose the issues with your collection and offer up a prescription for how to fix it. You don't need to start from scratch! What's at the core of this is working. The problems have to do with fit and proportion. Do you need to create new patterns? No! You need to take these existing pieces and retool them. You're going to make it work!"

And she did. Emma's collection was a success, and she learned so much from seeing it through.

If you look at the process of creating a work of art or a design as a journey of one hundred steps, steps one through ninety-five are relatively easy. It's the last five that are hard. How do you achieve closure? How do you finish it? That's the hard part.

MAKING IT WORK MEANS finding a solution to a dilemma, whether it's a senior-year thesis collection, a difficult boss, or a flat tire. When my students made it work, they reached a new level of understanding about their abilities to successfully problem solve, and that gave them additional resources when moving forward to the next task at hand. When we figure a way out of a tricky situation in our own lives, we learn something and gain confidence in ourselves. Making it work is empowering.

On *Project Runway,* the phrase serves as a constant reminder of the seriousness of our deadlines and of the finite limitations of each designer's material resources; in other words, when we return from shopping at Mood, that's it. Whatever they purchased is what they have to execute the challenge. If they discover that they're without some critical ingredient, then they're stuck, and it's "make-it-work" time.

There's a big difference between my relationship with my students and my relationship with the *Project Runway* designers. When my students were in a jam, I could tell them what to do to get out of it. By decree, I cannot tell the *Project Runway* designers what to do, nor can I assist them in any way other than through words. I learned this the hard way.

During Season 1, Austin Scarlett was having difficulty threading one of the sewing machines. In my then state of naïveté, I sat down at the machine to help. After all the years I've spent around designers, I can thread a sewing machine with my eyes closed.

Within seconds, one of the producers called me out of the sewing room.

"What are you doing?" she asked. "You can't do that."

"It's just a sewing machine," I said. "It will take me one minute to fix."

"But if you do that for Austin, then all of the other designers will expect you to do it for them," she said. "And if you don't, then it may be perceived that Austin had an unfair advantage."

I hadn't thought of that. She was right. I had to let go and watch the designers struggle. It took a little while, but eventually I got used to this new role as a hands-off mentor.

But I still enjoy being a hands-on instructor whenever I get the chance. I love how fresh young minds are, and I love watching them grow to take in new information. It's so satisfying to see them come out the other end of the school year more sophisticated and closer to knowing what they need to know in order to accomplish their goals.

Truth be told, I never dreamed that I would become a career educator. In fact, it's ironic, because growing up I hated school. And I do mean *hated*.

Don't misunderstand me: I loved learning. As a child, I always had a million creative projects going on at home. But I hated the social aspects of school. I was a classic nerd with a terrible stutter. I preferred the sanctuary of my bedroom, and I was crazy about books because they transported me to another time and place (one far less oppressive than Beauvoir, the National Cathedral Elementary School in the 1960s, I can assure you). I was also crazy about making things: I was addicted to my Lincoln Logs, Erector Set, and especially my Legos.

I would spend almost all of my weekly allowance on Legos. And in my youth, Legos weren't packaged in the prescriptive way they are now; they came as a bunch of anonymous blocks that you would purchase according to size and color, plus doors, windows, and, later—be still my beating heart—roof tiles.

As you can probably imagine, between my stutter and my fetishizing of Lego textures, at school I was taunted and teased. I knew that I wasn't one of the cool kids, and I never tried to pretend otherwise. I was always the last kid picked for games at recess. (Perhaps it's no wonder that I hate, loathe, and despise team sports even to this day.)

My big macho FBI-agent father, George William Gunn, was J. Edgar Hoover's ghostwriter, and he not entirely happy about the oddness of his only son. He coached the Little League team and did everything he could to get me on a sports field. It was a disaster. I was bullied. I was beaten up.

Looking back, it seems like having a tough-guy father would have been helpful, but the truth was, he really never seemed to understand me, so we never had much of a relationship. And oddly enough, even when he knew I was getting pummeled at school, he didn't teach me how to fight back. He never once said, "Let me show you how to sock someone."

The result was that I was a terrible fighter. I thought I was going to be a concert pianist (yes, I was every kind of nerd), so I would not hit for fear of breaking a hand. That meant I was a biter and a hair puller. If you got into a tangle with me, that's what would happen. You'd get bitten and have your hair pulled. I wouldn't even know what I was biting. I would just be in a frenzy, biting anything I could get a hold of.

An interviewer once asked me, "Who would win in a fight, you or Michael Kors?"

"Oh, that's easy: Michael Kors," I said. "Because I'm a hair puller, and he barely has any hair. There's not enough to hold on to."

When I was older and had to declare a sport, it was swimming. I loved swimming primarily because it's solitary—that and you don't sweat. (My sense of propriety was off the charts even back then.) Furthermore, I was good at it, especially the breaststroke and backstroke. In an unexpected and extremely appreciated show of support, my father took up coaching the swim team.

So I had swimming and my grades to be proud of. I also had the piano, which I studied for twelve years and became quite good at, but there was no reason to share that tease-worthy tidbit with my classmates. And yet, I was flailing. What was I going to be truly good at? What would it take to prove to my peers that I did in fact have value other than as a punching bag? For a long time I had no idea.

My teaching career began in an innocent enough way. When I was twenty-five years old, a former and much beloved teacher, Rona Slade, invited me to be her teaching assistant for a summer course for high school students at the Corcoran School of Art (now the Corcoran College of Art), one of the nation's last remaining museum schools and my alma mater (class of '76).

They really care about craft there. The Pre-College Intensive Workshop met six hours a day, five days a week, for a month. Rona and I had a great time and played off each other well. I felt proud that I could help someone for whom I had so much respect.

At that point I was a financially strapped sculptor who made ends meet by building models for architecture firms in Washington. Although I enjoyed model making, it wasn't very lucrative when one factored in the vast amount of time required to make each model. I was probably making about a dollar an hour.

But I loved sculpture. One of my favorite artists is the sculptor Anne Truitt. When I first saw her work in 1974, I was transformed. It was like the first time I saw a painting by the abstract expressionist Mark Rothko. I felt physically lifted off the ground. I've always thought the reason Truitt wasn't as well known as she deserves to be is that she doesn't easily fit into any particular genre—neither in the Washington Color School nor the Minimalists. There's not a box to put her in, so she gets lost. I was so lucky later to study under her and then to speak at the opening of her posthumous retrospective at the Hirshhorn Museum and Sculpture Garden in 2009.

In any case, when Rona asked me to stay on at the end of the summer of 1978 to work at the college, I jumped at the chance. The position would include teaching a three-dimensional design course as part of the first year of studies. Furthermore, it was full-time, which meant that it came with benefits. Even better, it paid a whopping $6,000 per academic year. Needless to say, I was ecstatic.

But then, when it got closer to my start date, I was terrified.

I realized I had no idea how I would fare in the classroom without Rona at my side. Would I be teased as I had been in grade school? Would the students throw paper planes and spitballs? Would they tie me up and hurl me out the window and into the parking lot? The more I thought about it, the more gothic the scenarios became, and the more I was struck mute and paralytic with terror.

Attempting to drive to work on that first day, I found that I was incapable of pushing down on the accelerator. I sat for a good ten minutes or so before I rallied sufficiently to get the car to move. When I arrived in the school's parking lot, directly across the street from the White House, I got out of the car and . . . promptly threw up on the asphalt.

Ah, the dawn of a glorious career, I thought, *vomiting in front of my new place of employment.*

I washed up and walked dizzily into my classroom to greet my new students. I found that the only way that I could appear to be even remotely composed before them was to stand with my back braced against the blackboard, because my knees were shaking so badly that I knew I would topple over without the wall's support.

I would like to tell you that the next day was better and that the day after that was better still, but that would be a lie. This same horrible scenario of fear and sickness was repeated for several days in a row.

Finally, I gathered up enough courage to share my terror with Rona. I was sure she would tell me I should quit immediately. But instead, she said very matter-of-factly with her Welsh accent, "Oh, I'm familiar with this malady. It will either kill you or cure you. I'm counting on the latter." And she smiled tenderly, my very own Florence Nightingale!

Indeed, it cured me—eventually—and I was able to make it through the year without dying or passing out in front of my class. And the students didn't throw airplanes or hurl me out the window. From then on, I was even able to keep down my breakfast. Talk about *make it work*!

I'm not built to be a public persona, but through sheer force of will, I've made myself step up to the plate. I'm really fortunate. I had parents who believed in education and a mother in particular who nurtured and fostered culture in our home. She wanted her children exposed to as much as possible. We went to museums all the time. We read books. I wasn't born with a silver spoon in my mouth, but I was extremely lucky, because in our home education and exposure to culture were everything. Either one can help you through life.

Everything got better when I became a teacher. I found an apartment and moved out of my parents' house. I was part of a new community and made new friends.

The only sad thing was giving up my sculpture studio, which I'd long shared with the painter and my dear friend Molly Van Nice. In fact, I gave up sculpture altogether. I thought I was going to miss it, but I found that the teaching experience was creative in its own way. It was so thoroughly satisfying and rewarding that I no longer felt the need to make my own artwork.

Within the hallowed walls of the distinguished institution in which I worked, it was the precedent that one practiced what one taught. Rona did not. She had been a textile artist, but she was no longer engaged in that work. I decided to embrace her as my role model, and even though my not being a practicing artist or designer raised some eyebrows, I thought: *I'm not apologizing for this. And I'm not pretending that I'm doing something that I'm not. Besides, I can always return to sculpting if I hear the call. It's not going anywhere.*

One spectacular experience from my time teaching at the Corcoran was a classic "make-it-work" moment. In late October 1979, the school received a call from the White House requesting that our students make original ornaments for the Christmas tree in the Blue Room. The president at the time was Jimmy Carter.

My reaction: How exciting! The catch was that we had a mere week to create everything, because whoever had made an earlier commitment had backed out, or perhaps had made something horrible and unacceptable. (We heard a rumor that the Jimmy Carter White House perceived the work of this original ornament maker to be "inappropriate," and we had a wonderful time trying to imagine what in the world those ornaments had looked like.)

In any case, who would say no to this request? Debate about how to get this done ensued. There was a lot of talk about making this a special project and inviting the participation of any interested students and faculty. Many people were against leaving this important task up to young people. But ultimately it was decided that my second-year Three-Dimensional Design students were up to the challenge. As an enhancement, a class of ceramics students would make "wrapped packages" for under the tree. Fantastic! We charged full steam ahead. And we made our deadline!

Our ornaments were stunning. We chose a folk art theme and, using balsa wood, created the most elaborately beautiful shapes and forms—musical instruments, animals, pieces of furniture, and buildings—including a miniature White House that allowed you to peer inside and see miniature rooms.

But, oh, we were so very, very delusional. None of us had a grasp on the size of that tree. We carefully walked our boxes of meticulously wrapped ornaments and ceramic packages over to the White House, navigated the security and X-ray process (security opened each and every wrapped ornament, which took hours), and were eventually escorted to the Blue Room.

The tree was at least as big to my eyes as the one at Rockefeller Center. As I continued to stare at it, it became bigger still, like the magical tree in *The Nutcracker*—only more like a giant redwood than a ceiling-brushing pine. And its scale was exaggerated by a formidable scaffolding of many layers that encircled it and went up to the ceiling. We had enough ornaments, I figured, for a hedge out back.

Indeed, as we started hanging, the tree quickly consumed our works of art. We looked through the boxes hoping there would be some giant ornaments we'd forgotten, but no. We were toast.

So what were we to do? We had to make it work. Our reputation as an academic institution and our individual reputations as artists were on the line.

I left and drove to Sears Roebuck on Wisconsin Avenue, because I had recently been there and had seen a Christmas display that included life-size bright red lacquered Styrofoam apples. Sure enough, I found piles of boxes containing a dozen each. I took all of them to the register and asked if more were in stock.

No.

Could they be ordered from another store?

With this question, the sales associate began to look at me

differently, as though I were operating a bootleg Christmas apple operation and would be selling them out of a truck in the parking lot at twice the price.

"They're for the White House!" I finally blurted out, with both pride and panic.

This got her attention. The next day, we had fifteen hundred stunning red lacquered apples for the tree. In fact, we had too many. I enjoyed giving them as gifts with the message: "Almost made it onto the White House Christmas tree."

Our folk art creations stood out brilliantly against the enormous cone of glistening red lacquer. It was a masterpiece. We'd made it work!

Let me add that the Iran hostage crisis was going on at the time, which generated a huge amount of Sturm und Drang and loads of extra security.

Let me also add that Mrs. Carter was kind enough to pose for an official White House photograph with each of the students and then with all of us as a group. After the holidays, we hadn't received the photos, so I followed up with the press secretary and learned that there had been no film in the camera (imagine: the predigital era!). The photographer had not, alas, made it work.

NOW FOR A MORE modern example of making it work: *Project Runway*'s entire Season 6 was plagued with problems from the start. You may remember that as the year we saw a battle over who would get the show: Bravo or Lifetime. While taping the season, we were in a period of suspension, not knowing how the lawsuit would be resolved and, therefore, not knowing our network destination. Also, it was our first season in L.A., and we were all adjusting to being out there. Luckily, all the producers of the show have been fantastic, and everything worked out for the best.

I've heard that a lot of people were disappointed when Gordana Gehlhausen and Christopher Straub went home in the last challenge. I see their point, especially when it comes to Gordana. In fact, it's the only time I've ever heard what the judges were planning and gone up to Heidi Klum and said, "Are you sure this is the way you want things to go?" Not because there was anything wrong with the three who went to Bryant Park: Carol Hannah Whitfield, Althea Harper, and Irina Shabayeva (the winner). They are all incredibly talented young women with great futures ahead of them.

But there was not a lot of diversity represented. I was sad about that from a design perspective and from a home-visit perspective. Remember, I had to go to each of these people's homes and hang out with them and their families. It just seemed very one-dimensional to have them all be women in their mid-twenties and relatively well to do. I asked Heidi, "Are you really certain? The homogeneity bothers me."

It didn't bother her or anyone else, so what can you do?

Season 7, by contrast, was glorious all the way through, and I think the best year so far. We returned to New York, and Michael and Nina Garcia were able to be part of every episode.

The talent was amazing, and even the eccentric characters were appealing in their own way. Seth Aaron Henderson, the Season 7 winner, is a very caring, thoughtful guy. He has a wife and two children. If you took his wife and son and daughter and lined them up in their house in Washington State, you would say, "This is a classic American family." Then you bring him in and you think, When did the circus come to town? And his mother-in-law lives in the basement, which seemed a little Freudian. His children even said he's like a kid himself.

Mila Hermanovski, Emilio Sosa, Jay Nicolas Sario—all of them, too, were very gifted.

But even that blissful season had its wrinkles.

Now that there are sixteen designers a season, it gets hard to follow. I never was able to tell the two twentysomething brunette designers, Janeane Marie Ceccanti and Anna Lynett, apart, lovely as they were. I kind of miss it being just twelve. At the reunions, you find yourself saying, "Who are all these people?"

Season 2 had a preliminary episode called "Road to the Runway," which introduced everyone. I loved that, and I hope we do it again sometime.

More frustratingly, two of the best designers, Emilio and Jay, seemed to have disdain for me. They rolled their eyes at everything I said. The show is edited to look like I'm in the workroom just once or twice a challenge, but I'm there all the time. It was a lot of scorn to soak up.

Their attitude was something of a shock. I said to one of them, "I feel an obligation to each of you, and an aspect of that is to give you equal time in the workroom. But if you don't want it, we can talk to the producers. We can say that you actively don't want me engaged with your work, and you will never again see me at your workstation."

But they kept having me there, and it began to hurt. I thought: *What did I do to offend you? It's my job to talk to you about your work. I have a lot of experience. Why won't you let me help?*

One time Heidi made the workroom rounds with me. Jay acted like she was the Second Coming. He oohed and ahhed over everything she said while continuing to give me the cold shoulder.

I said to him, right in front of Heidi, "I wish I had that kind of response from you. I guess maybe Heidi should do these workroom visits instead of me." Heidi looked at me, clearly thinking, *Whoa, what's been going on here?*

But I couldn't hold back. I was really pretty upset by the whole thing, and as much as my feelings were hurt, my sense of what's appropriate was, too. My feeling is that people should want to be nice, but even if they don't want to be, they should fake it, because being abusive to someone who's deeply involved in the industry you hope to excel in just makes no sense. What do they get out of making me, or anyone, into an enemy?

I'm not saying this in any kind of threatening way. I just think the more friends, or at least friendly acquaintances, you have in a small world like fashion, the more opportunities are likely to waft your way. If you get a reputation for being a diva, you'd better be truly phenomenal to overcome the personal bias people are going to have toward working with you.

Sometimes there is direct payback. In Season 5, I was made a judge for one episode, and a lot of people saw that as a kind of revenge for Kenley Collins's being so dismissive of my opinions throughout the season. Well, that wasn't the thought behind it at all, and I was very much against judging. In fact, from the start I begged the producers to keep me out of the judging chair. And I'll never, ever, ever do it again, but I did learn a lot from the experience.

Here's how it happened: I was at Christian Siriano's show and received a call from the producers asking me if I could fill in the next day as a judge because Jennifer Lopez had backed out at the last minute. I begged them to find someone else. I said if they made me be a judge, I'd have to go back to the workroom that night and say I couldn't engage with the designers as they finished up their collections.

I am always with the designers for the five hours before the show at Bryant Park, and I thought that I couldn't spend all that time backstage if I was then going to be judging them. It wouldn't be fair, I said, for me to wear two hats like that, to potentially guide them toward choices that I would then judge them on. It would appear duplicitous and potentially corrupt.

Plus, there were the personal biases I'd built up from spending so much time with the designers. I said to the producers, "You know I have a terrible relationship with Kenley. I don't like her work and have been very vocal about it. Her not winning could become a self-fulfilling prophecy on my part. It would look bad, and quite frankly, it would be bad."

My arguments had no effect on them. So I said, "Please do your very best to find someone else. If at the very last minute you need me to sub in, I will do it, but I beg of you to find someone else."

They promised they would move heaven and earth to find someone else and so spare me from having to judge.

The next morning Heidi comes up to me and says, "Okay, we need you."

"No, you don't," I said. "It's you and Nina and Michael. What's wrong with three judges?" (Yes, I had thought about it all night.)

Well, Heidi was so wonderful. I just love her. She is such a strong, smart woman. She said, bluntly, "What's your problem with this?"

"I have a relationship with these designers. In the case of Kenley I have a really bad relationship," I said. "I don't sit in judgment of them in this manner."

"Are you telling me that in all your years of teaching you couldn't separate your students' work from their personalities?" she asked me. "And you couldn't evaluate their work independent of who they were as people?"

Well, that left me speechless. She had me there. How was this different from an academic environment in which I had to spend a year with these students and then grade their work? I looked at her and stiffened my back and said, "You're right. I can do this!"

And things happen for a reason. I learned that I was in fact able to separate my personal feelings from my judgments. I also learned a great deal about the designers' work that I never could have known just from seeing them in the workroom.

Most significantly, before that moment, I'd never had a chance to evaluate the work off a dress form, aside from the flurried moments during which I escort the designers and models from the workroom. In the workroom, it's always static. When the models come in for the fittings, I'm not there. When I come in afterward to ask how it went, every one of the designers says, "She looks great in the clothes!"

(Which reminds me, I'm always perplexed when they switch models. You know your current model's size and shape. Why would you switch? It only makes your challenge more difficult.)

So to be at the judging and to see the clothes move—or, in the case of Kenley's work, not move—on models was really transformational for me. I learned to wait to pass judgment on things. I used to tell the producers what I thought of the garments as soon as the models left the workroom for the runway. But from Season 6 on, when the producers would ask me pre-runway, "What do you think? Who are the top three?" I would respond, "I'm not saying a thing until I see it on the runway. You just can't tell until you see it move—or not."

The World Owes You . . . Nothing

YOU MUST BE JULIE!" I greet my companion, a twelve-year-old girl who, with her mother, is joining me for lunch at Saks Fifth Avenue's café to benefit a great charity.

The pair has donated a great deal of money to the charity in order to dine with me. I am flattered and excited to meet my young fan and her mother.

"It's *Julia*," the young girl says, her voice dripping with disdain.

"Oh, I'm sorry," I say, taken aback by her haughty tone. "I was given the wrong name. In any case, it's wonderful to meet you!"

I immediately have a bad feeling about this lunch. Julia is petite and very skinny. I hope her chinchilla shrug is fake, but she tells me it is real. She's wearing platform heels and a miniskirt, and she's sporting lots of makeup. And she's wearing a real diamond pendant, as she feels she needs to tell me.

She says she goes to an elite private school chosen for the fact that there is no dress code. She never wears the same thing twice, she brags.

I express shock that she has that many clothing options.

"Well, she styles them differently," her mother qualifies.

I confess that I rather enjoyed wearing a uniform myself, because there's something very democratizing about everyone wearing the same thing at that age. No one feels the urge to compete.

"There is no competition!" Julia says, scoffing at the thought. "No one dresses better than I do."

"I can see why you're trumping all your classmates," I say, pointing to her Prada handbag.

"Oh, this is a cheap thing," she says, referring to what I assessed to be a $1,500 bag.

"I only believe in expensive clothes," her mother says by way of explanation.

Julia is no longer a fan of mine, I'll tell you, because I don't wear bespoke suits. I don't have a private plane. I don't go hobnobbing with stars. I don't have a car and driver. She registered her extreme disappointment with each of these revelations.

Well, our food arrives, none too soon. But as soon as the waiter sets down Julia's food, she waves her hand and says, "Away." When asked for an explanation, she just says, "No."

The chef, sweet as can be, comes out and asks her what is wrong with what he's prepared. He seems eager to fix any problems.

"Drama," she says.

Seriously, that is her response to this generous man.

The waiter takes the plate back and does something to it. When it comes back, she picks at it desultorily.

She had horrible table manners. Her hair was falling in her food. She loudly imitated a cough she heard across the dining room, causing everyone to stare at our table in horror.

Then I learned the purpose of the lunch: Julia wanted to

be a judge on *Project Runway*. "Call them," she instructed me. "Tell them I have to be a judge."

"That's going to be a tough sell," I said. "Other than wearing clothes, I don't see that you have much experience with fashion."

"That's why I'd make the perfect judge," she insisted.

"Clearly, you are talented," I said. "Which of your talents do you value most?"

"Meanness," she said without hesitation. "I'm really good at it."

"Our judges are not *mean*," I replied, trying to keep from losing my patience. "They are honest and fair. They care about good work and innovation."

She didn't seem to be processing what I said, but I tried once more to get through to her. As they left to go shopping at Saks, I made a suggestion.

"You have so much and are so lucky," I said. "Maybe you should take some of the money you're planning to spend today on shoes and give it to refugees?"

"I would never do that," she said, laughing.

"Do you know about all the displaced people and the suffering?" I asked. (The news at the time was full of reports of displacement, death, and starvation.) "What's your reaction to that suffering?"

She tilted her head back and said—I kid you not—"Let them eat cake."

Young Julia was the most distressing example I've seen to date of an overblown sense of entitlement, but the phenomenon is pretty far-reaching, especially in the fashion world.

And it's not just rich girls who are displaying such a detachment from reality.

In my later years of teaching, I started to see a disturbing trend: students who couldn't function without their parents' help. They were so overpraised and so overprotected that they were incapable of handling any problem, whether it was dealing with a teacher they didn't like, sharing space with a roommate, or struggling with a class for which they didn't have an affinity.

We would actually get calls at the school from parents who wanted to negotiate their grown children's grades for them. Luckily, we had a system in place whereby the student would need to specifically grant his parents permission to speak to the administration. Many students denied their parents' requests. But some of the students actually thought their parents getting involved was a good idea!

One of my most talented students had a certain arrogance about her that rubbed a lot of people the wrong way. During her time at Parsons, we had a Designer of the Year competition, and this student assumed the winner would be she. I still remember her tearful fit in my office after the results were announced.

"It was supposed to be me," she said, crying.

"By whose reckoning?" I asked.

"Mine, my family's, and my teachers'!" she shouted.

"With all due respect to the faculty," I said, "this is the decision that was made."

"It should be reconsidered," she said.

"No, it shouldn't be, and it won't be."

Viewers got a glimpse of such a drive to win from Irina Shabayeva of Season 6. When I did the home visits, I learned a primary source of her ambition. Her mother scared me to death.

"My daughter will win this," Irina's mother told me, as if it were a statement of fact.

"Well . . . ," I said, nervously. "There are three extremely talented people in this competition—"

"She. Will. Win," she said, staring deep into my eyes.

Oh, to have that kind of confidence!

Maybe it's because I became a public person late in life, but I have never lost the belief that all my success could vanish just like that. I count my blessings all the time, and I pick my battles. I've heard some people didn't want to see *Project Runway* go back to Los Angeles for Season 8 and tried to get me to advocate for us to stay in New York, but these things are far bigger than I am. Heidi lives in L.A., so she loves the idea of staying close to her family. Where we film is totally not my call. I always say: "If I get hit by a bus tomorrow, believe me, the show is going to go on."

This sense of humility does not appear to be universal. Whenever I'm out in public, there are certain people who make demands of me as if I owe them a huge debt—even though we've never met.

Not long ago while I was walking down Columbus Avenue a woman leaped out of a car.

"You have to meet my daughter!" she shrieked. "She's thirteen! She has to be on *Project Runway!*"

I explained that the show has very strict rules and that the young lady couldn't be considered until she was twenty-one. This made no impression on the girl's mother.

"Rules are meant to be broken!" she insisted.

I've finally learned how to respond to these overeager parents. At an event for young fashion designers, a husband and wife accosted me. They appeared dragging a small float behind them. It held miniature dress forms with outfits on them, and at the back of the float their fifteen-year-old daughter sat in a chair. I was the honored guest, so I couldn't flee, much as I wanted to. They gave me this entire sales spiel about the daughter. I listened politely and responded, "Clearly, she has talent and ambition, but she can't be on *Project Runway* until she's twenty-one."

They weren't buying it.

"You're robbing her of her stardom!" they said. "She's a prodigy!"

"Okay," I finally said. "Let's play this scenario out. Your daughter gets on *Project Runway*. She wins."

They're nodding excitedly.

"Then she returns to her junior year in high school. How do you think she'll feel?"

That question stopped them dead in their tracks. They hadn't thought that far ahead. I said, "If your daughter is this sensational now, think what a few more years will do for her. Think of how much stronger she will be. She's only going to get one shot at it. Why not save it up?"

It's like learning a musical instrument. If you're thirteen and a classical pianist, think of how much better you will be at eighteen or twenty-one, providing you keep practicing.

The parents seemed disheartened, but those are words to propel you forward rather than to crush your dreams. Isn't it nice to have things to work for and look forward to, especially if you're so young?

Stage parents make me crazy. They're dogged and determined, but it reaches a point where it's cuckoo. I find it very unsettling.

IT'S EASY TO BLAME parents for bad behavior, but there's plenty of culpability to go around. Teachers are not totally innocent, either, when it comes to encouraging talented students' sense of entitlement. Too many of us so overprotect our students that they don't develop a sense of the logical consequences for their behavior.

A faculty member at Parsons who taught there for many years was in a state of apoplexy because she believed that she had to give a B minus to a student in her Studio Methods (garment construction) class. She asked me to counsel her on how to stomach giving such a low grade to someone she thought had so much promise.

"What are the conditions?" I asked.

"The student hasn't turned in most of her assignments," she said. "She hasn't been to class. But what she has turned in is excellent. She's extremely talented."

"She hasn't been to class? That doesn't sound like a B minus," I said. "That sounds like an F."

"But she's a good student," the teacher said. "She communicates with me via e-mail."

"You need to fail her," I said. "But I'll make a deal with you. If you give her an F and she appeals the grade and makes up the missing assignments, I'll allow you to raise it to a D. But only if she appeals the grade and makes up the work."

The teacher took my advice and gave the absentee student an F.

As I expected, we never heard from the student. Ever. So the F stood. And we all learned something: The teacher wanted the student to succeed more than the student did.

People send each other messages all the time through their behavior, and the message here was, Fail me. I don't want to be in school anymore. Instead of admitting that she wanted to get out of fashion, she forced the faculty to make her decision for her. From a faculty member's point of view, I have this refrain: Why should I want you to succeed more than you do?

PEOPLE WHO ARE USED to having everything done for them don't often have a strong grasp on how the real world functions. Sometimes it's infuriating. Other times it's kind of adorable.

Case in point: One night in 2007 I was at Gen Art's Fresh Faces in Fashion event. Gen Art is an incredibly valuable organization that supports the work of rising artists and designers. In addition to running myriad events and competitions all over the nation, Gen Art features the work of selected rising fashion designers at an annual event in New York. I was asked to judge the Best in Show, along with Diane von Fürstenberg and others.

Diane and I were there early, though she thought that she was late ("Even when I'm late, I'm early," she declared). To kill time, we toured the displays in the lobby of the Hammerstein Ballroom (a relic from a bygone era of New York nightlife), which featured the work of rising accessories designers. Cocktails were in abundance. While I declined, Diane gave me reason to believe that she had not.

"I need a hot dog," she announced to me in her languid voice.

I wondered for a moment if that was a euphemism. *Don't look at me,* I thought.

But no, she was speaking literally.

"Why is there no food at these things?" Diane asked me. "They fill you with booze but give you nothing to eat. Do you think there's a hot-dog vendor on the street? Oh, and I haven't any money."

This struck me as a little odd. Remember, this is *Princess Diane von Fürstenberg*, now divorced from the prince and married to a member of American royalty, the billionaire Barry Diller. She had a car and driver sitting out front. Surely there were a few dollars in there for tolls and such? But no.

"Don't worry," I assured her. "I can treat us each to a hot dog. Let's see what we can find outside."

We exited the dusty old ballroom. Diane lunged forward to inform the driver of her shining, bottle-green Bentley that we were going off on a hot-dog mission. I looked around and saw nothing that remotely looked like a vendor's cart. However, I knew that there was a diner at the corner of Thirty-Fourth Street and Eighth Avenue, a nice little dive called the Tick Tock.

We sashayed down the sidewalk, Diane's arm wrapped around mine. I held the diner door for Diane to enter, and she burst in as if she expected silver trays filled with every kind of hot dog and condiment to greet her. Something told me that she had never been in a place like this before. Sure enough, she didn't seem to know how diners worked.

While I tried to catch the eye of a waitperson so we could sit down, the famished Diane grew impatient. After sighing heavily, she called out to the rather cavernous space, "I need a hot dog! Someone, anyone, please bring me a hot dog!"

Well, this captured everyone's attention. Every waitperson and every diner was suddenly staring at us. Imagine how we must have appeared: me in my Tim Gunn outfit and the ever-recognizable Diane von Fürstenberg (no wallflower, she) in all of her stunning regalia.

An amused waitress approached and led us to a booth just

to the right of the entrance while Diane kept repeating, "I don't need to sit. I just need a hot dog."

"Well, let's sit for a minute," I cajoled, winking at the waitress. "Maybe you'd like some french fries as well."

"Oh, yes, that would be nice," she said, and smiled with a look that suggested she could smell them, "and some onion rings, too!"

Onion rings? Maybe she had been in a place like this before.

"Oh, and some pickles!" she called after the waitress.

Pickles? I began to suspect DvF was a diner junkie.

Diane's energy was low, I could tell. She has a languorous look that I find extremely sexy, but in this case it looked more like a low blood sugar haze. I asked the waitress if she could bring whatever food was ready first as soon as possible. She obliged by bringing the pickles right away. Diane began to perk up as soon as she took a bite.

We talked and laughed and when the hot dogs, french fries, and onion rings arrived (quite speedily!), Diane had two bites of the hot dog, a couple of French fries, and then didn't even touch the onion rings.

When we got up to leave, the people in the next booth leaped to their feet and asked whether they could take a picture with us. I'm always game and was about to oblige, but Diane stepped in and held her hand up.

"I'm sorry, darlings," she purred, "but we're late for an event where we're both needed very badly. We don't have time for a picture, but here, have some onion rings!" And she handed her stunned fan the basket.

I'm not sure what the moral is here . . . I really just wanted to tell that story. But maybe it's that declaring to a room full of strangers, "I need a hot dog!" won't get you what you want no matter who you are, unless you follow protocol and sit down and order like a regular person.

Also: If you're going to yell demands for food into a room full of strangers, you'd better be as fabulous as Diane von Fürstenberg if you expect to get away with it.

I SEE DETACHMENT FROM reality all the time on *Project Runway*. It's often about three weeks in that the designers become daffy with exhaustion. We shoot each season in thirty or thirty-one days, and something weird always happens on Day 24, every single season. It's the point of the cycle at which everyone gets annoyed with one another: designers, judges, crew, and producers. Everyone starts complaining about how they need more sleep. Fights break out. Also, everyone gets into magical thinking.

On Day 24 of Season 3, for example, Angela Keslar very somberly approached to ask me a question that was plaguing her. There was a lot of buildup to that meeting. The producers told me that Angela had come to them with questions, to which they responded, "You have to hold your questions for Tim and ask him on camera."

Well, we went to Mood, and I'm reminding the designers of how much time they have, and she says, "Tim, I have a question. We're all really tired and really stressed out. And I'm sure you'll say no, but can we have an extra fifteen minutes?"

"You just answered your own question," I said. "What do you think?"

"No?"

"No," I said.

Out-of-touch behavior is certainly nothing new to the fashion world. I have an infinite number of less-than-endearing stories where it morphs into outrageous divadom. I'll share a couple of my favorites with you. Both are about people who work at that bastion of the industry, *Vogue*.

In the summer of 2006, a writer named Robert Rorke called to interview me for a *New York Post* story about *Project Runway*. He asked me, "Of all the things you've seen since you've been in the fashion industry, what's the one thing you will never forget?"

And I said, without hesitation, "That's easy. Anna Wintour being carried down five flights of stairs from a fashion show." He said, not surprisingly, "Tell me more," and I told him what happened. He ran only one line about it, but I'll tell you the extended version, including the ridiculous epilogue.

I was at Peter Som's show at the Metropolitan Pavilion on West Eighteenth Street. It was held on the fifth floor, and there was one large freight elevator. Knowing Anna was a Peter Som fan and knowing she famously dislikes riding in elevators with other people, I thought, *How will she ever get down?* I didn't have a seat so I was standing, coincidentally, in a place where I could see Anna sitting in the front row with a bodyguard on either side of her.

An announcement is made—"Ladies and gentlemen, please uncross your legs"—which they do so the people in the front row won't accidentally trip the models walking by them and so the photographers' shots aren't obscured. Anna is the only one who doesn't uncross. Her foot's sticking out there ready to put some unsuspecting model into the hospital. But anyway, the show ends. The models survive. And as the lights come up, *bam*, Anna's gone!

I was there with a colleague from Parsons, and we had been discussing the will-she-or-won't-she-take-the-elevator question, so we ran over to the elevator bay to see if Anna would deign to get on. She wasn't there. Then we looked over the stairway railing. And what did we see but Anna being carried down the stairs. The bodyguards had made a fireman's lock and were racing her from landing to landing. She was sitting on their crossed arms.

I ran to the window to see if they would put her down on the sidewalk or carry her to the car like that. They carried her to the car. And I thought: *I will never forget this.*

So the *Post* printed the following version of that story on July 9, 2006, a day that will live in infamy: "After leaving a fashion show held in a loft building with only one freight elevator, Gunn wondered how the *Vogue* editor, who doesn't ride with mere mortals, would get downstairs. 'Her two massive bodyguards picked her up and carried her down five flights of stairs and then—I looked out the window—they carried her into her car.'"

I didn't think anything of it, but then the next day, Monday morning, Patrick O'Connell, *Vogue*'s director of communications, called and left a message that I was to call Anna Wintour right away. I was too scared to call her back that day, but on Tuesday I called Patrick and was told, "Hold for Ms. Wintour."

Forgive my language, but I'm thinking I'm about to have diarrhea, I'm such a wreck.

He comes back on the phone and says, "I'm terribly sorry. She's unavailable at the moment."

"I can't handle the suspense," I said. "Can you please tell me what this is in regards to?"

"Yes," he said. "She wants you to have the *Post* print a retraction of your statement."

"That would imply it's not true," I said.

"It's not true," he said.

"It's very true," I said, "and I can tell you exactly when it happened." Thankfully, I keep a diary. I looked it up and told him the exact date, time, and location.

"Oh dear, oh dear, oh dear," he says. "I'll get back to you."

There are then many more phone calls, each one insisting upon a retraction or at least an apology. I refused.

"I didn't malign her character!" I insisted, and still do. "My statement was a matter of fact."

"Ms. Wintour knows how to work a Manolo," Patrick finally said, angrily.

"Is that what this is all about?" I asked. "If you want an apology from me, here it is: 'I apologize if I implied that Ms. Wintour doesn't *know how to work a Manolo*.' The goal for her departure from the fashion show was clearly speed, and that's what she received from these bodyguards. Furthermore, I wasn't alone in seeing this. Dozens of people saw it."

In his next call to me, he said, "We're going to have to get the lawyers involved."

By this time I am not only a ball of anxiety, I'm also spitting mad. I said, "Well then, you'll please permit me to get some corroborating witnesses."

As luck would have it, that afternoon a fashion executive was in my office. He asked me why I looked so distraught, and I said, "I've been through hell. That *person* over there at *Vogue* is threatening me over a quote in the *Post*."

I told him the story.

There was a pause, and then he burst out laughing. "I was at that show!" he said. "I saw exactly what you saw!"

He grabbed the office phone and called Patrick right then. Just like that, my nightmare was over. He told Patrick that he, among many others, could attest to the by-now-infamous stairs story. After days of torment, I was off the hook.

But I knew Anna still must have been seething, so I decided I was going to take the high road. I called Richard, the florist I use, told him the basic situation, and asked for a fabulous and tasteful arrangement of all-white flowers to be sent to her office. I got on the subway and delivered a card of my stationery, on which I said something like, "I apologize if my comments in the *Post* caused you any unrest or unease. It was never my intention. With respect and regards, Tim Gunn."

There was never any acknowledgment, but I felt like I'd done everything I could to put the matter right. And thankfully, I never heard a peep about any of this again. When I met Patrick in person sometime later, I told him, "I am so happy to see you. I was afraid that Anna had hurled the floral arrangement at your head and you were in a coma somewhere. It's good to see that you are alive and well."

He laughed, and I felt like I had closure on the whole ordeal. But it made me think that perhaps the devil really does wear Prada. I couldn't believe how sweet she seemed in that great movie *The September Issue*. Of course, she did know the cameras were on . . .

When Times Square was shut down the day before New Year's Eve in 2009, I suspected it was something inside 4 Times Square, which houses *Vogue*. As in: She huffed and she puffed. Although it turned out to be a suspicious unmarked van, there exists on that corner a more constant source of fear.

UNFORTUNATELY, THE REST OF the *Vogue* staff follows in her Manolo footprints when it comes to haughtiness.

On September 12, 2006, I was on a panel at the New York Public Library with *Vogue*'s André Leon Talley, as well as the photographer Timothy Greenfield-Sanders and *People* Group's Martha Nelson. I don't know how much the audience learned about fashion, but I certainly learned a bit about how ridiculous people can get when they live in the fashion-world bubble.

André Leon Talley arrived with a sizable entourage. And this was not a large greenroom. The NYPL's director of public programs, Paul Holdengräber, a lovely guy, comes in and says, "We'd like to have a sound check."

We're all filing out to go do the sound check and André says, "I don't need a sound check!" and he stays with his crowd of hangers-on. Fine. The rest of us do the check. Everything sounds great.

When we return to the greenroom, we see that someone has spread a translucent barber's bib over André and he's reclining, his arms at his sides. He's being fed grapes and cubes of cheese one by one, like a bird in a nest.

I can't believe we're witnessing this, I thought.

Well, the best was yet to come.

André is cleaned up. The bib is folded. It's time to go do the panel.

"The room has been cleared," André says. It's not a question; it's a statement.

"Cleared of what?" Paul says.

André clarifies that he means of people. Apparently he doesn't like to walk down the aisle of a full auditorium; he prefers it be empty.

Paul is in shock. He says, with a bit of a tone, "Empty? It's standing room only. We have no place to move these people *to.*"

The room starts to get tense.

"It doesn't matter," I interject. "We don't have to walk down an aisle. There is a stage door."

"Why didn't anyone tell me?" André asks in annoyance.

"I'm telling you now," I said, "and if you'd come to the sound check, you would have known that, too."

At the panel, André made a lot of very bizarre pronouncements. Someone in the audience asked why larger-sized women weren't represented on designers' racks or in magazines. "Obviously, I'm a large woman," she said, "and I feel like I'm not marginal, although I think that large women are marginalized."

It's a good question, and a common one, but André began praising Mo'nique. "I think there's no woman more fashionable than Mo'nique," he said. "I love Mo'nique. And I think that Mo'nique does for the full-figured woman what Rosalind Russell used to do in those wonderful 1950s Technicolor films, and I love Mo'nique, and I say that seriously. That show she had for the large woman, the contest, I thought that was really wonderful, and I always think she's great on her own show. I think she's wonderful."

I couldn't stay quiet any longer. I tried to tell the woman something useful about sizes in the industry and was glad when Martha Nelson agreed with me.

"Yeah," she said, "let's be real."

At the end of the panel, I let André and his crew go first in the elevator so I wouldn't have to ride up with them. I just couldn't handle another moment with him.

Well, I thought I'd seen everything, but then walking through the freight exit on my way to the subway, I pass André's Maybach parked *in the freight room.* Apparently, he couldn't even walk from the sidewalk.

Don't get me wrong: *Vogue* is an essential read for all fashion lovers. Anna and her team are very talented, and they are on the cutting edge of trends. But when I see what a bubble they're all living in, how detached from reality they are, how much money and time is wasted in the course of their work, I worry about the example it sets for people coming up in the fashion world, a world that—let's face it—is now a lot more crowded and a lot less moneyed than it has been in years past.

I hope that *Project Runway,* which encourages hard work, thrift, and skill, is part of the solution to that unsustainable excess and hauteur. I am heartened that, by and large, the thousands of young designers I come into contact with are simply trying to make beautiful things to the best of their ability, rather than attain a lifestyle that allows them to be bibbed and hand-fed grapes.

And yet, maybe not. I thought the recession would have more of an impact on the industry, but there's still a fleet of limousines over there in front of 4 Times Square.

I look forward to seeing what the next generations of fashion designers and magazines look like. Between the demise of so many publications and the decline in fashion company fortunes, I wonder whether we're heading for a new age of decency and diligence. I would certainly rather the industry not go broke, but if that's what it takes for everyone to acquire some values and lose that sense of entitlement, maybe a little belt-tightening wouldn't be so tragic.

Take the High Road

I DON'T KNOW IF PEOPLE have gotten ruder or if my tolerance level has declined. I recently spoke to a group of high school juniors and seniors at the Cooper-Hewitt National Design Museum's Teen Design Fair. Those young people are our future, and I believe in them. I love being part of the annual event.

We had a Q&A afterward, and one of the teens stood up and asked what advice I had for them.

"I'll give you some life advice," I said. "The first piece is: Listen and listen *intently* when you're being spoken to about something. The second: Take the high road. When presented with frustration or anger or discontentment with a situation or a person, don't reduce yourself to that level. Don't get into a conflict in that moment. You'll feel better about yourself for it."

Well, to my surprise, this created a near frenzy in the room. The students were aghast. I was surprised by the reaction, so I said: "Tell me more about why that seems like bad advice to you."

"I believe I should stand up for myself!" said one student.

"I'm not saying you shouldn't stand up for yourself," I said. "I'm just saying, in the heat of the moment, walk away from it."

One episode of *Project Runway*'s Season 6 speaks to this. The challenge was for each designer to do a look that complemented his or her best look on the show to date.

Althea Harper thinks Logan Neitzel is copying her zipper-collar design and complains about it to her own model and to Irina, whom she mistakenly thinks is her friend. She starts to get worked up, but then she thinks: *You know what? I need to concentrate on getting my own work done and let this go.* She takes the high road and doesn't say anything.

In the end, Logan gets voted off because his garment just wasn't very good. On the runway, Irina borrows Althea's words about Logan and turns them against Althea. Irina suggests that Althea has copied *her* by doing a sweater. Heidi disagrees, and Irina is embarrassed. In the end, Althea wins the challenge.

One moral might be not to trust Irina—and not because she's a bad person at all, because she's not. She's just incredibly tenacious. But the true lesson, one that I hope I eventually convinced those design students of, is that taking the high road is always the best way to go. You feel better about yourself, and the world feels better about you.

That doesn't mean it's always easy. After a recent plane trip, I was standing at the baggage carousel. I'd been waiting a rather long time for my luggage. In fact, no one had gotten any suitcases at all. A rumor started that our bags were lost. This is, of course, very stressful, but I figured getting all worked up would make it only more stressful. But one of the women who'd been on my flight did not agree. She started pacing and trying to recruit an army to storm the airport administration:

"Let's all go together to the office and scream that we're not going to take it anymore!"

I turned to a passenger standing next to me who seemed tempted to follow and told her, "Don't even think about it. Take the high road."

Sure enough, a short time later our bags showed up and no one had to handcuff herself to the ticket counter. There are times for protest, for civil disobedience, but on a day-to-day basis, it's best to avoid bringing out the big guns.

And yet, I know for a fact how hard it can be to keep your frustration to yourself. Sometimes keeping in feelings can be painful. One time, for me, it proved almost fatal. I was in my twenties and was having an excruciatingly horrible lunch with my mother, during which I honestly saw my life pass before my eyes.

Fortunately, I arrived at the restaurant, Clyde's of Georgetown, first, because waiting just fuels my mother's innate sense of martyrdom (unfortunately, this trait is genetic). Also, if she gets there first, my mother will often hand the hostess her credit card as she walks in to avoid a discussion at the end of the meal about who will pay the bill.

"You just love taking the battle out of this thing, don't you?" I ask when I learn she's done this. (Twice, I've actually gone to the hostess and substituted my credit card for hers, but then it turns into a real fight.)

When she arrived, I greeted her with a hug and a kiss, which was like hugging and kissing a mannequin, because she was as stiff as an ironing board. I love my mother dearly. I'll miss her when she's gone. She is filled with emotion and cries during commercials, but she's never been very affectionate with her children. She doesn't kiss me. I hug her, but she doesn't hug back. I don't doubt how much she loves me, but she's kind of like a rock. Make that an elegant rock: Nancy Gunn has always been the spitting image of Queen Elizabeth II.

I always wonder if her lack of demonstrable affection is connected to an incident from her youth. My grandmother liked to tell the story of coming home to find the goldfish were dead. When asked what happened, my mother answered, "I don't know. I just took them out of the bowl to kiss them."

Was it then she learned that a kiss can kill?

In any case, we were shown to a table. I think we both ordered a glass of wine (and if we didn't, we should have), and I chose the restaurant's famous hamburger.

When the food arrived, Mother was carrying on about something about me that was annoying and irritating to her. It could have been anything from not calling her in a month to "I told you that I hate that tie, so why do you persist in wearing it?"

I nodded, eating, attempting to take the high road and pretending to agree with her, but unfortunately, I was internalizing my frustration. Suddenly, I inhaled a too-large bite of burger. I couldn't breathe. I couldn't eject it from my lungs. I literally thought I was going to die. I started to gesture wildly.

My mother thought I was simply behaving badly, so she carried on talking and looking at me disapprovingly. Thanks to the ringing in my ears as I started to suffocate, her voice grew silent, as did the ambient voices and clatter in the large room. Panic set in. I was going to die—right there, upright in a chair, with my elegant mother carrying on and on throughout the speedy evolution of my death.

For some unknown reason, my panic abated, and resignation set in. It was at that moment that my constricted throat

muscles relaxed and the potentially fatal chunk of chuck cata-
pulted from my mouth—and landed in my mother's lap.

She was horrified and said so. "What the hell is the matter
with you?" she hissed. "If you're angry at me, just tell me so.
You don't have to spit your food onto me!"

"Spit my food onto you? I almost died! Right here! In front
of you! I thought I was going to die, and you're embarrassed?"
I yelled back. "Wouldn't you have been more embarrassed by
a corpse?"

By now I was in tears, and Mother looked contrite. She responded, "Don't be ridiculous; you didn't die. You're here."

I asked for the check.

Mother said, "I'll take it."

"No, I will," I retorted. "Because if I had died, then you
would have *had* to take it."

We never did resolve whatever conflict we'd been having,
but at least my near-death experience changed the subject.
And I learned a couple of valuable lessons. One: When you're
on death's door, rules of etiquette should most definitely be
suspended. And two: Never try to resolve an emotional conflict
over food. I recommend ordering drinks instead—with neither
ice nor olives.

In the absence of choking hazards, taking the high road is
a good strategy. You never know where the people you're dealing with today are going to be in twenty years—or next month!
Even if you're a really selfish person and are only looking out
for your own self-interest, you should treat people well. Why
bitch-slap someone unless you're leaving the planet for good?
Don't burn bridges; you might need those bridges later.

But there are limits. You don't let yourself be abused. Even
as you take the high road in a perilous situation, you should try

to figure out how to keep from being in a difficult position like that again.

For years, my refrain was: I bend and I bend and I bend until I snap. No matter what was dished out I would think: *Keep taking the high road . . . hmm, it's getting awfully high . . . the altitude's really something . . . I'm having a little trouble breathing . . .* Then I would basically have a nervous breakdown.

Now I've learned to set limits and to take cues from people's behavior.

For example, if someone is always late to meetings with you, you need to ask yourself why you continue to let yourself make appointments with this person. If you hate doing something for someone, you need to ask yourself why you keep doing it.

I used to host a wonderful fashion scholarship dinner. I did it for five years in a row. But the last time I did, it was horribly managed. Every decision made around the event was terrible, and the people organizing it were completely dismissive of every concern I had. I just hated the whole thing.

So I said to myself, "Why am I doing this?" I thought, *This is something I was doing to be nice, and it's no longer fun to do, so I'm going to bow out for next year and let someone else host.*

I gave the organization a lot of notice and felt very liberated.

But I wasn't free yet. The group's president took me to lunch, and he was horribly abusive, telling me how angry he was that I'd stopped doing the event and piling on other complaints about me for good measure! Then he followed up with threatening e-mails. He was just furious that I wasn't going to host his event anymore and figured he would try to intimidate me into reconsidering my resignation.

I thought, *Well, I'm definitely not going back after being talked to like this!*

When someone else from the organization contacted me, I explained how badly I felt I'd been treated. He must have said something to my tormentor, because then I received this syrupy e-mail from the yelling president about how much I mean to the event. He asked me if we could get together again.

I thought about it for a second and then said, "No."

This was an abusive relationship. *If I return to the event,* I thought, *I am condoning this bad behavior.* It sends the message that it's okay to talk to people cruelly. And it just isn't.

You don't want to behave badly back at people like that, though God knows it's tempting. But you also don't want to put up with mistreatment. It does no one any favors.

The abuser could be your boss, and in a case like that you just need to try to keep your integrity, even as you're being mistreated, and try to get out of the situation as soon as you possibly can. Now that I've been on television, though, it's like the whole world is my boss. Everyone has an opinion they want to share about my demeanor on my shows, or who the *Runway* finalists were, or all manner of things over which I have little control. And truth be told, a lot of these people don't even seem to know who I am. They just know they've seen my face before. I've found it's always good just to smile and walk away. Or, in the case of nutcases, run away.

Usually people think of me as a surprisingly nice person as fashion people go, but occasionally someone will corner me on the street and say: "You're so mean!"

Often this is because people mistake me for Clinton Kelly from *What Not to Wear*—which I'm sure would disturb him to no end, because I could be his grandfather. When I determine that's the case, I say, "I think you have me mistaken for—"

Then they'll interrupt and say, "I've been watching that show for years!"

And I will say, "Then you really should know I'm not Clinton Kelly."

During the *Project Runway* Season 3 auditions, which were held at Macy's, I went into Au Bon Pain every morning to get a coffee and a croissant. The first day, the woman behind the counter pointed to me and said, "Look, it's Michael Kors from *Project Runway!*"

I didn't want to disappoint her and I didn't think it mattered, so I just took the high road. I smiled at her and said hello and thanked her for watching the show. But the third morning, she got closer and said, somewhat concernedly, "What happened to your nice tan?" Finally, I told her I was the other guy on the show. She seemed so confused that I almost regretted not having done my best Michael Kors impression and told her, "Good call! I gotta get back to the beach."

WHEN I WAS LITTLE, I had a great uncle who was verbally abusive. I've never forgotten a particular dinner he ruined with his bile. I still remember the tone of his voice at that holiday get-together, even though this was easily fifty years ago. I remember the room, what people were wearing, the candles, and then the excuse people kept offering one another: that he was ill. It didn't make a difference to me. If he was going to be that nasty, why didn't he stay in bed?

I also have vivid memories of people behaving kindly.

My godparents, Earle and Suzanne Harbison, who are

thankfully still alive and well and live in St. Louis, have always been so good to me. When I think of them, it warms my heart.

When I was first in New York, they always used to come to town and take me out for big, delicious dinners. I was so grateful, because I was struggling on my teacher's salary. Well, usually they would have me over to their hotel for a drink beforehand, but one time I said, "You've never seen my apartment. Why don't we have a drink there this time?"

This was early in December. They came over and were lovely and talked about how nice it was at my tiny little place. They were incredibly gracious about every ratty piece of furniture and beat-up pot and pan. I lived paycheck to paycheck and wasn't able to save anything, much less to furnish my apartment properly. But it was cozy, and I loved it.

Well, I received a Christmas card three weeks later from my godparents, and in it was a check for $10,000. That money at that point in my life changed everything for me. I was able to get some decent housewares, and I had a financial cushion for the first time in my life. It was a godsend.

Wow, I thought when I saw all those zeroes on that check, *they were really horrified by the apartment!*

Though I think that was part of it, mainly I think they just wanted me to feel secure. They are wonderful people who really looked out for me, and they wanted to do what they could to make my life easier and happier.

In my own godfathering I've done my best to imitate their concern and generosity.

It hasn't always worked. My mother took the family to Disney World twice. The first time we went, my niece, Wallace, said in a pseudo-whisper to her mother, my sister Bub (her real name is Kim, but I have called her Bub or Bubby since she was born and I couldn't say "baby" correctly), "Don't worry about me, Mom. You have your hands full with Mac [her brother] and Uncle Nag."

"What did she call me?" I asked, horrified. "Uncle *Nag?*"

Noting my annoyance, Wallace turned to her mother, nodded in my direction, and said: "See?" She was seven or eight.

It was a good reminder that I needed to be more fun with the kids. I've tried to be good to them and to put whatever skills I have at their disposal. I always used to make my niece's Halloween costumes. My favorite was the year I transformed her into a Life Saver.

My mother is a huge pessimist and often says, "If everything is fine, then I'm pleasantly surprised." Years ago, my mother seemed to take great relish in predicting a doomed marriage for my sister: "It will most certainly end in divorce—soon!"

My sister has been married to her husband for more than thirty years. She's never complained about him once. They are totally committed to each other. My mother thrives on the negative, so her daughter's happy marriage is a big missed opportunity for complaint. That's no way to live.

After all, why would you choose to be the angry great uncle in the corner rather than the beloved godparent with the long and happy life?

RULE 4

Don't Abuse Your Power— or Surrender It

O NE DAY WHEN I was working in academia, I had to get some things postmarked by five, and before they went out they needed to be signed by a senior administrator. At three, I knock on her door, but she's in there with a young woman. I'm told to come back. Finally, it's four and we're about to miss a deadline, so I open the door and peek in.

The administrator is standing behind a girl, lifting her arms up and then pushing them down, and yelling, "Serve from the left! Take away from the right! Now you do it! Serve from the left! Take away from the right! More vigor! Serve from the left! Take away from the right!"

The girl was practically in tears.

I gathered she was preparing for a fancy dinner and the girl was going to be serving. It was a little terrifying. I gathered my signed papers and scurried off to the post office, rather traumatized after witnessing this borderline abusive enforcement of dining etiquette.

This was a rather horrible example of the Bad Boss, a type with which I am far too familiar. To wit: Once we were having

{ 57 }

a staff meeting, and the boss said, "I've decided we need a café au lait at the front desk."

"That's nice of you to consider the coffee needs of the visitors," I said.

"What coffee needs? I'm talking about a light beige," she corrected me. "A charming English major out of Howard University."

My jaw dropped. These are the kind of outrageous racial remarks we were dealing with in the seventies. It happens even now, but back then it was particularly prevalent and grotesque.

Which reminds me: In circumstances like that, you have to say something. It isn't bad manners to point out when someone is being gallingly racist. You have an obligation not to let it slide. Alas, why is it that childish, bigoted, or foolish people so often seem to wind up in charge?

One of the worst bosses I ever had was a producer on *Guide to Style*. He always wanted to make sure everyone knew he was in charge, so he would assert himself in very aggressive ways.

In Episode 2 of Season 2, the adorable Gretta Monahan and I were doing the reveal of our subject's new look to her family and friends. Well, the soundstage was unbearable. It was 120 degrees, and there was no air circulation. The model fainted. I caught her and then heard, from the audience, the boss say, annoyed, "Well, we've got to do it again!"

I followed him into the production room and said, "This can't continue. We have seven more hours. This is abusive. We can't go on like this. You can do whatever you want to me, but not to them. The crew and the audience are suffering. They didn't sign on for this." The walls were paper thin, and everyone knew something was going on because I never walk off the set. When I got back, the crew gave me a round of applause.

But it wasn't over. The producer ran onto the set and started yelling at me.

"*They* signed on to this!" he yelled, pointing to the audience while poking me in the chest.

"Can we please not do this here?" I asked. I don't like to fight in front of the crew with anyone, much less our boss. He ignored my request and kept poking.

"They signed on to be guests," I said, "but not to a sensory-deprivation environment with no water and 120-degree temperatures."

We fought until we had no fight left in us. The model revived. We got through it somehow. But I thought: *I am never working for this man again.* And I never have. One day my wonderful assistant told me, "I have your old boss on the line. He's at Ralph Lauren and wants to buy you a suit?"

"Hang up on him," I said.

At the same time that I see people wielding power badly, I've seen a backlash against holding power of any kind, and I just don't get it. For example, I don't understand that be-a-pal parenting style. Children don't need more friends. They need parents. You're the adult, and they need you to act like one. And if you think you want your child to be your friend, you need to be in therapy.

Dale Carnegie wrote an insanely popular guide for salesmen called *How to Win Friends and Influence People.* It has been in print for something like seventy years, and it contains stories about how to become a better conversationalist. It's basically about how to trick people into liking you.

In one of the book's illustrative stories, a man is told to

run the refreshment booth at a fair. He arrives to find two elderly ladies disgruntled because they feel their power has been usurped. So he hands one of them the cash box to manage and asks the other to show the teenagers how to use the soda machine. This supposedly gives them a sense of power and control and ensures that "the evening was very enjoyable."

This is supposed to be a happy story, but it doesn't sound like a good idea to me. You were in charge. You were handed the cash box. You're new. The person running the event was a veteran. There's probably a *reason* why those ladies weren't in charge.

That kind of behavior guide is all about giving insecure people something to make them feel good about themselves. But it's so patronizing.

In another story in the book, a student in a beginning crafts class asks to go into the higher class. The teacher agrees. Everyone's happy, and a lesson has been learned about "our deep desire to feel important."

Well, I don't know about that.

During my time as chair of the Fashion Design Department at Parsons, too many of my students would say on the first day of school, "I'm more advanced than this class. I need to take a junior rather than a sophomore class."

I always responded, "We have four weeks to add/drop. I'll speak to your faculty, and they will know within a month if you are so adept that you can go to the next level."

Did it ever happen? Never!

In *Life's Little Instruction Book,* which has sold more than ten million copies, the writer advises us to: "Compliment three people every day."

Well, maybe, but only if they're worthy. And do you keep a checklist?

"Buy great books even if you never read them."

"Own a great sound system."

"Sing in the shower."

Really, it's like: "Act aggressively happy whether you are or not."

A lot of that book is about busting out of social constrictions and getting all touchy-feely and feel-goody. Well, I think a lot of people feel entirely too good about themselves and bust out of social constrictions entirely too much.

My now twenty-three-year-old niece, Wallace, much matured from the "Uncle Nag" days, often picks me up here in New York City and then we take the train together to see the rest of our family. I adore my niece, and I am so impressed with her great manners. She is so respectful of people. She sends thank-you cards. It's great fun to do things with her and to have her visit because she's good company and seems genuinely to appreciate a dinner out or whatever we choose to do together.

Also, the visits are planned well in advance, so there are no surprises. (One of the cardinal rules of visits: *Don't drop in.* People who drop in drive me to despair. It's simply not acceptable.)

People need boundaries and rules. Society does, too. You don't flourish if you're left to do anything in any situation. I say this about art and design all the time, and it doesn't always make me incredibly popular.

A few years ago, I was at a conference of fashion design educators in Copenhagen. I was the only American, and I was reviled because I was from *that place*. What they hated about

American design was that we look at design through a lens of commerce. They thought it constrained creativity. I maintain that having constraints is very helpful for the creative process.

On *Project Runway,* the designers do better work when they have a very specific challenge. And for me, it's easier to discuss their work when there's a real point of departure, rather than the do-whatever-you-want challenges, when all I can say is, "Well, if this is the look you wanted to achieve, you did it!"

With a certain amount of maturity, we can set up our own constraints. That's a lot of what education is about—letting people set those assignments for us so that when we graduate we can start to set them for ourselves. Even now that I'm in my fifties, I still face certain situations where I have to admit that I need some rules to help me figure out what I should do.

Bosses should think of themselves as fulfilling this kind of boundary-giving function that school and parents do. They need to be clear about expectations and rules so everyone knows when an employee is doing well or not doing well. And when expectations are not met, there should be logical consequences, whether that's the loss of the job, a decrease in salary, or something less drastic. There is no reason, in any case, ever to yell. And yet we've all seen it: bosses who lose their tempers constantly.

What I want to know is: What makes people abusive to their underlings? I don't think people are born that way. Is there some role model for people who tells them this is the way they get to the top? Did Donald Trump's "You're fired!" catchphrase corrupt them?

My suspicion is that cruelty to those you have power over is insecurity, pure and simple. These bad bosses are afraid if they're too nice to people, they won't be taken seriously.

As anyone who sticks around in an industry for a while knows, the people who have the best careers and the best lives (and often who do the best work) are not the demanding, screaming, flinging divas. They're the people who take their ego out of it and put all that energy into their creative life.

I remember in Season 2, we went to see Fern Mallis, who runs Fashion Week here in New York and worldwide, too. I think it was Daniel Vosovic who asked her, "What's the one piece of advice you'd give a young designer getting into this industry?"

"Be nice," she said without hesitation.

I thought: *God bless you, Fern Mallis.*

I'm sure some people thought she was joking or being flip, but she was dead serious, and dead right.

There is absolutely never any reason to be a fire-breathing dragon.

I would say this to faculty who yelled at their students: "You hold all the power. Do you think there's a single student who questions your authority? Even if they do, you're assigning them a grade. There's no reason ever to raise your voice, to threaten, to storm around. You're not competing for power; you're holding it, all of it."

When people have a choice between two similarly talented people and one is a drama queen and the other is responsible and friendly, whom are they going to pick?

Everyone wants to work with people who are low maintenance. You have a huge advantage over the competition if, in addition to being a talent, you are easy to work with.

I'd never met a fashion prodigy until Christian Siriano. He's probably the most talented person who's been on the show so far. But that's not why I agreed to do the foreword for his 2009 book, *Fierce Style*. I did it because I respect and like him, and I want to support the careers of people who are both talented and decent to others. Christian has all of the attention and success necessary to create an unbridled diva, but he's not, and I don't believe he ever will be. Wisely and correctly, he knows that divadom will not advance his career.

If you got rid of everyone in the fashion world who was high maintenance, there wouldn't be that many people left. But even if you're in a crazy world like that, it doesn't mean you have an obligation to drop your standards of behavior just to fit in.

Again, that doesn't mean being a doormat. In twenty-nine years of teaching, I often had times when I had to have sit-downs with my students, but I did so calmly. I would say, "Look, things are not going well," and explain what needed to change. If the students took what I said seriously, we all had a great time and they learned a lot. If they didn't, then they got bad grades and we all moved on with our lives. That's all you need to do.

Parents can take a lesson from this, too. The ones I know who are rough with their children are always saying, "I want them to know who's the boss!"

Guess what? They do know. You're going to be the boss or the mom or the dad whether you're good or bad at your job. The kids or workers may be pushing your buttons, but you can say, "You are pushing my buttons, and I want you to please stop it!" Or you can recognize that that's what's happening and take a break and try to get over it.

The same thing goes for pets. I'm a huge dog lover. I grew up with wirehair terriers, an English setter, and the aforementioned sad-sack basset hound, Brandy.

I love a mutt. I tend to look at purebreds these days a little differently than I used to. They seem to have so many health problems, and then the vet just says, "It's in the breed." It's like royalty who used to inbreed and whose progeny ended up with three eyes.

Anyway, when babies cry on the plane, I never think it suggests bad parenting. But when dogs bark constantly, I tend to think it's bad dog-raising.

I live next door to a loud West Highland terrier that barks all the time. Luckily, I can't hear it through the wall, but I can from the hallway. That to me doesn't seem like a happy animal.

I blamed my sister and her husband for the fact that their yellow Lab barked all the time and couldn't even sit on command. I had sessions with the dog whenever I was there to try to teach her tricks, but I didn't visit frequently enough for the training to stick. Ultimately, I realized the dog was in fact quite smart. Her attitude was, I'm not going to sit if I don't have to!

When I was a child, we had an English setter that was a real handful. She ran away all the time and would occasionally bite my sister or me. One Thanksgiving Day, my grandmother was stirring gravy, my mother was basting the turkey, and my sister and I were ambling around the kitchen. The dog was missing yet again. Then, suddenly, the dog burst through the screen door with a rabbit carcass and proudly used it to knock over everything in the room.

"Aw," I said. "Look, she's brought food for Thanksgiving!" I was very little.

Does anyone remember Barbara Woodhouse's 1982 book *No Bad Dogs: The Woodhouse Way?* We bought it to help us with our terrier Raffles. Within an hour of the book's purchase it had been devoured—by the dog.

When I was a child, I took Brandy for obedience training. She was great through the entire thing, but on the day of the exam she sat down and would not budge. I yanked at her so hard I pulled her collar off. Still, she wouldn't take the exam, and we failed. That meant we couldn't get the certificate of completion, and I really wanted it, because both our names were on it and I wanted proof that I'd worked hard. So I took her back and did the whole thing again. Once more, she was brilliant all the way through, and then, at the exam, she sat down and wouldn't show her stuff.

Well, I bawled my eyes out from disappointment, but eventually I came to realize that she just liked the social activity of it all. Dumb like a fox, she thought: *If I keep failing it, he'll keep bringing me back!* Well, twice was enough for me. And the truth is, she was impeccably behaved when she wasn't being tested, so obedience school wasn't a waste, even if I didn't get that piece of paper.

Some people tell me I would be a good parent because I am able to stay so calm even when designers are behaving like sugared-up toddlers all around me. I'm always flattered when people say that to me, especially because I love children, and I like to imagine I'd be good at raising them. But maybe it only seems that way because I'm not actually a parent. With my students, I could walk away and go home at the end of the night to my own cozy apartment. Everyone's a great parent if they don't have kids.

I do feel very protective of children, though, and frequently fear for young people I encounter with parents who tolerate— or, more often, model—insane behavior.

The scariest instance of this was one day when I saw a mother literally putting her children's lives at risk.

I left my dentist's office in New York's Greenwich Village and walked west to Sixth Avenue. I waited at a red light as cars passed along. At the corner beside me was a woman with two small children, one of whom was in a stroller. To my shock and horror, the woman entered the path of moving traffic using the child's stroller as a battering ram with the full intention of crossing the street no matter what.

The older child, her daughter of about four, was by her side, but the onslaught of traffic clearly frightened the little girl to a point of total paralysis. She stood in the middle of the street while a car screeched to a halt a mere foot from her. Her mother, now successfully across the street, returned to her, yanking the now sobbing child by the arm, yelling, "When the sign says 'Don't Walk,' it means *run!*"

I was shaken by the incident and felt bad that I hadn't done anything to stop it. Should I have run to the child's rescue? Should I have scolded the mother?

As a nonparent myself, I never want to assume I know better than a child's own mother or father, but sometimes even those of us without kids can identify dangerous behavior. The parents I have relayed this story to agree that it seems pretty psychotic. They also typically enjoy the following story, about the ultimate in permissive parenting.

I was walking home on Broadway from the Ninety-sixth Street subway station. It was one of those rare summer nights in the city when the temperature is bearable, the humidity low, and sweet air wafts in from Central and Riverside parks.

All the restaurants with sidewalk tables were full and boisterous. Everyone was happy to escape air-conditioning.

A few blocks from my apartment, I saw a young boy of three or four walk up to a table of al fresco diners. He greedily grabbed some pasta with red sauce off one stunned woman's plate and proceeded to eat it with both hands.

The boy's mother spoke to her son about the incident, but not with the admonition that I was expecting, which would have gone something like this: "Stop! What are you doing? That is not your food! Apologize to these diners at once. You are in trouble, young man!"

Instead, she took a napkin from an empty table, wiped his hands, and said, "Darling, if you like that, then we'll go inside and get some to take home." She never even acknowledged the diners!

Every time I walk by that restaurant, I wonder, Where are that mother and son right now? I would say this child was doomed to grow up to be a social outcast, but it's altogether possible he will grow up to be a star. I see a lot of similarly terrible behavior on sets.

A celebrity who shall remain nameless announces to an underling, "I'd like a Diet Coke. I want a twelve-ounce glass and five ice cubes, each no bigger than three-quarters of an inch in length." Once the Diet Coke arrives, the celebrity says, "These ice cubes are at least an inch, and I count six. This is unacceptable." And *fling!* He throws the drink across the room.

In academia, too, you see this kind of outrageous behavior. I knew a dean who had soup delivered to his office. I once saw him bring a spoonful up to his mouth, scream, "This soup isn't hot enough!" and hurl the container across his office onto a wall, which I noticed already had stains on it.

Is this really happening? I thought. But I was glad I saw it, because if someone had told me the story, I would say it couldn't possibly be true.

What enables this kind of behavior? What allows people to think that they are permitted to behave that way?

Don't even get me started on Isaac Mizrahi. In my view, he's one of the world's biggest divas.

One time, Isaac threw a fit about a security guard from the second-floor showroom at Liz Claiborne Inc.'s Times Square offices. Why, you may ask? Was he stealing? Harassing guests? Showing up late? No, *he was wearing brown.*

Can you imagine having your senses so offended by something that it provokes such an extreme reaction?

You just never know what's going to set people off. One time when I was on Martha Stewart's show, she visited me in the greenroom. I threw out my arms to embrace her, but in lieu of a greeting she asked with a tone of horror, "Who let you in here with that?" She pointed to the Diet Coke I was drinking.

"No one," I said. "Someone brought it to me."

"W-what?" she stammered. "I don't allow Diet Coke in this studio. It's not to be anywhere around me. I'm going to find out who's done this."

And she stormed off. Then later she made an off-camera announcement to her audience about how they shouldn't drink Diet Coke, either. She gave me a lecture in front of the audience about how bad Diet Coke is. Something about the chemicals? I couldn't even focus on what she was saying because of how vehemently she was saying it.

About a year later, I was at a table with colleagues from Liz Claiborne Inc. for an event at which Martha was the honoree, so I offered up my Diet Coke story. They didn't seem to believe me, and no one laughed. Everyone acted as if I'd made it up.

Later in the evening, Martha, while at the podium, pointed

to me, and said, "Tim, I see you're here! I hope you're not drinking Diet Coke!"

My table exploded in laughter because they had the bizarre backstory. I think the rest of the crowd was a little confused.

Now, while we're on the subject of Martha, who incidentally appeared in my first book as a fashion icon: Martha's daughter, Alexis Stewart, strikes me as one of the angriest people I have ever met. Alexis and I did a commercial together for Martha's Macy's line. Whoever was directing the commercial was wise enough to have Alexis and me do our lines together before bringing Martha in.

Alexis kept cursing under her breath in anticipation of her mother coming, saying things like, "goddamned bitch," almost as if she had Tourette's syndrome. I was shocked that she could be so disrespectful toward her mother in front of total strangers. I also found it deeply ironic that the domestic goddess seems to have such an odd relationship with her daughter.

Speaking of irony: The domestic goddess and her daughter were at the Four Seasons for Thanksgiving dinner in 2009. I read *Martha Stewart Living,* and I always love looking at her calendar and seeing all the things she's doing for Thanksgiving preparation: "Get the turkey" . . . "Make cranberry sauce." The truth in this case was "Make reservation" . . . "Put on fancy clothes." Not that I begrudge her a meal out. Sometimes even if you're as domestic as Martha you'd just as soon let someone else whip up the Riesling gravy.

But back to the commercial shoot. We were out on a sound set in Queens and they'd totally re-created Macy's Herald Square at Christmastime, right down to the last detail. It was magnificent. But when Martha first arrived at the studio, she took a producer aside and said, "I thought this was going to be a closed set. What are all these people doing here?"

"We're supposed to be at Macy's during the holidays," he said. "They're extras acting as customers. They're *shopping*."

Meanwhile, Alexis seems to be tensing up. I've always thought that having famous parents must be hard on a person, but there are ways around it: go into a completely different field, make your own way, change your name . . . anything to carve out a little space for yourself. But Alexis's world seems to revolve around Martha. And yet she has appeared genuinely furious at her mother every time I've seen her. There's something *Grey Gardens*–y about the two of them.

During one of our little breaks on the Macy's commercial set, Martha gestured to the piles of linens and towels from her new collection and said, "Alexis, any of this you want for your apartment, please take it. I want to give you a housewarming present." It seemed like a touching and generous gesture.

"I wouldn't touch a single solitary item of this crap!" Alexis said, glowering.

Well, it rolled right off Martha. I thought, *Yikes! She must get this all the time.*

Abuse of power really can go both ways. If you're a boss, a parent, or a child, it's best to wield whatever power you have over your employees, children, or parents wisely. If you can't be gracious, don't spend time together. There's no gun being held to your head that says you have to associate with people who make you crazy. My family may be a little eccentric, but I would never talk cruelly to them—and certainly not in front of other people.

RULE 5

Get Inspired If It Kills You

WHEN I WAS TEACHING at Parsons, I went to visit our New York exchange students who were studying in Paris, France. With an expectant smile on my face, I asked them how things were going. I was so happy for them. *How lucky they are,* I thought, *to have this glorious academic and cultural experience.* I expected to hear stories about their walking through the city at night, strolling through the Louvre and the Picasso Museum with a notebook, eating baguettes beneath the Eiffel Tower . . .

"Oh, it's so boring here," they complained.

It was a good thing I wasn't eating a baguette, because I can guarantee you I would have choked on it.

"Boring?" I spluttered. "You're in the middle of Paris! Dullness is of your own making. You are in one of the most spectacular cities on this planet. You should be ashamed of yourselves for even using that word. *Ashamed!"*

The last *Project Runway* home visit of Season 7, I had a similar, horrible encounter with the designer Emilio Sosa.

He lived in upper Manhattan, and so I said, "What's it like having the Cloisters in your own backyard?"

If you don't know, the Cloisters is the branch of the Metropolitan Museum of Art devoted to medieval art and architecture. It contains thousands of works of art, including some of our most incredible ancient textiles, such as the Unicorn Tapestries from the fifteenth century.

"I've never been," Emilio asserted, with what I perceived to be pride. "I don't believe in anything that has to do with religion."

I confess, I am not at all religious myself, but I had to grasp onto a support to keep from toppling over with incredulity.

"Every corpuscle of every society in the history of this globe has religion at its core!" I brayed at him. "We're not talking about converting. We're talking about walking a few blocks to look at some of the greatest art of all time. Why would you shut yourself off like that?"

I love New York City and am so inspired by it. It's a magical place to me. Even when it's muggy and gross and the subway stinks, I am completely captivated by the city and find new things to love every day.

Walking to the subway one day on my usual route, I saw an antique store I'd never noticed before. It had clearly been there for ages and I'd walked by it a million times, but I'd never noticed it. It was like it appeared magically. Then when I walked into my neighborhood Dunkin' Donuts for my morning coffee, the woman behind the counter smiled and asked, "Where have you been?"

I'd been out of town for *Project Runway* home visits for a few days, and this quasi-stranger had noticed and missed me. I'd missed her, too, as well as everything about this city. It reveals just enough of itself every day that I'm never bored and never overwhelmed.

The other designer who I thought didn't like me, Jay Nicolas Sario, really stepped it up with his collection, and he and I healed and repaired during the home visit. But things got worse with Emilio.

I did not like the collection. He just looked at me and said that I frequently told him things, and the judges told him the opposite.

"I have no expectation that you will do anything I suggest," I said, "but I'm only trying to help you. I see a matronly collection with problematic colors. If the judges don't see that, too, I'm going to wonder what's wrong with them."

Regarding the judges' and their critical opinions, my mantra is: *Chacun à son goût;* that is, it's a matter of taste.

Emilio is a very talented designer, but to me he seemed to lack inspiration, and in my book that is a cardinal sin.

OCCASIONALLY, WHEN I WAS teaching, I would have a student who would ask me, "How do I get inspiration?"

I wanted to respond: "Drugs? I don't know! Whatever it takes."

"I'm just not inspired," these *art students* would say to me.

I found it so shocking. What were they doing in art school if they didn't feel the call to create? It's a hard life, and there's very little money in it. They should have gone into another line of work if they didn't feel inspired.

"Well, how can I *find* inspiration?" they would ask.

"Look around you!" I would say. "Look out the window. Go for a walk. Go to a movie. Go to a museum. Go see a show.

Read a book. Go to the library. Take the Circle Line. Have a conversation."

That's one of the main things I look at when I interview designers being considered for *Project Runway:* their inspirations.

With each year of the show, I've learned more about what would work. Season 3 was a threshold where we no longer had clothes that weren't well made. Since then, it's all about the relevance of the designers' points of view. A lot of time people who are outstanding seamstresses will say, "How can you turn me down? Look at this craftsmanship." But that's not what we're looking for. We want people with real ideas.

In the auditions we see a lot of gimmicky clothes, with too many bells and whistles and zippers everywhere—things that turn inside out and become a tent.

"You can't do this on the show," I tell these designers. "You can't make a prom dress that doubles as a jet pack in the course of a one-day challenge." It's like someone who brings in intricate hand-knitted sweaters. You can't do that on the show. There just isn't time.

Coming out of Season 5, I became suspicious of people who didn't come out of a conservatory-type academic environment. They haven't been through a critique. They don't know that it's about the clothes, not about them. Kenley's a good example. She took everything so personally and wore her defensiveness on her sleeve.

Designers need to know what's going on in the fashion world. I'm always so shocked when a major name comes up and the designers don't know it.

We have a huge questionnaire that we have applicants fill out, and there are three sections that I flip to: Education, Job

Experience, and Favorite and Least Favorite Designers. Favorite designers usually include Chanel (often misspelled Channel), Alexander McQueen, John Galliano, and Karl Lagerfeld. (Is the distinction made between Lagerfeld's own collection and his work for Chanel? Rarely.) There are rarely any American designers on the list. I'm over being surprised because I'm so used to it. But I still ask them about it.

"Why are there no American designers in either best or worst?"

"They're dull," the contestants often say.

That's like saying all American food is bland. That can't be true, because there are so many different kinds, from hot wings to chicken-fried steak to New York bagels. The American design world has figures as different as Marc Jacobs, Donna Karan, Oscar de la Renta, Anna Sui, and Ralph Lauren.

"We're looking for the next great *American* fashion designer," I respond to the anti-American applicants. "How do you feel about that?"

It's amazing to me. When you probe and ask what they like about Christian Lacroix they say, "I love couture."

Well, how many jobs are there out there for couturiers? Almost none. So maybe you should have a backup plan? And as long as you live in this country, maybe you should be able to at least talk seriously about what's been done here in this world you're likely to enter.

Similarly, if the auditioning designer's work is executed brilliantly but there's nothing new or innovative, who cares? That's what I would say of portfolios that were full of copies of clothing that already exists.

I would say, "Who wants to see nothing but perfect technical prowess? You need to use that to say something that's unique to you. Look around you! You see . . . a pile of books, a cloud in the sky, a fireplace. How do you interpret any of that?"

Some students tell me, "I need a photograph as a point of reference."

You *think* you need a photograph! You just need to push yourself. Similarly, if you have great ideas, you have a responsibility to the ideas to present the work well.

The greatest compliment the show receives is that most of the people who try to get on *Project Runway* aren't in it for fame. They want their fashion brand to flourish. With the exception of Santino Rice, who is now a judge on *RuPaul's Drag Race,* the drag talent competition on Logo, no one's gone on to be a TV personality.

Speaking of Santino, when he was asked to do the *Project Runway: All-Star Challenge* special, I told the producers it was a huge mistake. "It's going to be *The Santino Show,*" I said. And it was. I love Santino, I really do, but I've never met anyone else who so completely sucks the air out of a room.

I don't enjoy people who think they have it all figured out, because *I* certainly don't. I like the idea of always learning. Always. If you're not learning, what makes you want to get up in the morning? Why wake up if you have it all figured out? People who coast are not having any fun. It's also dangerous. People around you are still working and pushing themselves. If you don't keep up, it doesn't matter how advanced you were when the race started—you're not going to win it.

WHILE TEACHING, I FREQUENTLY brought movies to my classes to share with my students, because they were important to me. They always inspire me, and maybe you'll enjoy them, too!

⟅ THE FIVE BEST MOVIES ABOUT FASHION ⟆

1. *Blow-up* (1966)

Michelangelo Antonioni's 1966 murder mystery is a spellbinding masterpiece set in London in the 1960s, which I consider probably the most innovative and provocative fashion era of all time. David Hemmings plays a photographer whose career is loosely based on that of David Bailey (an early leader in the field of fashion photography), and the stunning Vanessa Redgrave plays his muse.

2. *Funny Face* (1957)

This frolicking romp stars Audrey Hepburn as the ugly duckling turned swan, Fred Astaire as a fashion photographer loosely based on Richard Avedon, and the fabulous Kay Thompson as a fashion editor loosely based on Diana Vreeland. It's a great behind-the-scenes look at fashion magazines. Think *The Devil Wears Prada* set to music. And after seeing this movie, you'll always "think pink!"

3. *The Women* (1939)

This wickedly funny film paints a portrait of 1930s society women whose lives revolve around beauty treatments, luncheons, fashion shows, and one another's men. The script is laugh-out-loud funny, and the entire film is a great escape, especially when I'm feeling bitchy and want to have a cathartic experience. (But please don't waste your time with the 2008 remake. It's sad.)

4. *The Devil Wears Prada* (2006)

In spite of my adoration of Meryl Streep, I wasn't enthusiastic about seeing this film. I thought, *Will this movie really portray the fashion industry accurately?* In order to make myself go, I made a date with Grace Mirabella, the former editor in chief of *Vogue,* and Jade Hobson, another fabulous fashion editor. Then I started fretting about whether or not the film would make Grace uncomfortable. Meryl Streep's character is loosely based on Anna Wintour, who replaced Grace at *Vogue* under dreadful circumstances. Grace was as still as a statue during the movie, which made me nervous. When the lights came up at the end, I slowly turned to Grace, whose eyes met mine. I gulped. She broke into a wide grin and shouted, "I loved it!"

5. *The September Issue* (2009)

I was dubious about what this documentary could really offer up about the inner workings of *Vogue,* especially when it comes to that sphinx-without-a-riddle, Anna Wintour. Wow, was I impressed. R. J. Cutler's documentary is brilliant: it's insightful, funny, ironic, drama-filled, and a freak show like none other.

❧ THE FIVE BEST FEMALE STAR TURNS ❧

1. Judy Garland in *A Star Is Born* (1954)

In this bigger-than-life movie about the rise of a nobody Hollywood extra into the motion-picture industry's biggest star, Garland becomes seduced by a star (James Mason) who's a self-centered cad. Still, she marries him and stays by his side until . . . the end. Speaking of, there are few movies for which I've experienced the kind of welling of emotion that's triggered by seven words spoken by Garland: "Hello, everybody. This is . . . Mrs. . . . . Norman . . . Maine."

2. Barbra Streisand in *Funny Girl* (1968)

In this amazing musical, Barbra Streisand handles drama, comedy, musical numbers, and tear-jerking sentiment with equal aplomb, and she does it all better than any actress before or since.

3. Vivien Leigh in *A Streetcar Named Desire* (1951)

In Tennessee Williams's Pulitzer Prize–winning play, Blanche DuBois says: "Nobody sees anybody truly but all through the flaws of their own egos. That is the way we all see each other in life." Ever the method actor, Marlon Brando reportedly stayed in his brutish character even during filming breaks, much to the disgust of Vivien Leigh. When she called Stanley an "animal," it must have come from the bottom of her heart.

4. Rosalind Russell in *Auntie Mame* (1958)

Rosalind Russell was born to play the madcap Mame in this story of an eccentric, fast-living society woman of the 1920s determined to "open doors" for her adoring nephew. Mame exposes him to everything from bootleg gin to oddball characters—all the while doing battle with her nephew's ultra-conservative trustee, who is equally determined that the boy's life remain free of "certain influences."

5. Faye Dunaway in *Mommie Dearest* (1981)

This movie is my number one guilty pleasure when it comes to movies. Yes, it is camp, but like they say, they don't make 'em like this anymore. A virtual facial contortionist, Dunaway plays up every scene and mood change. She's also able to act the part of the Hollywood diva very well. And this movie is full of diva behavior. Take, for example, the scene in which she chops up the rose garden, dressed in haute couture, the side of her face bruised and cut. She mutters "box office poison," and makes her unfortunate small children haul away the wreckage. Plus, she wields an axe like nobody's business.

❦[FIVE MOVIES I JUST LOVE]❦

1. *Valley of the Dolls* (1967)

"So you come crawling back to Broadway . . ." That's just one of a myriad of oh-so-quotable lines from the cult classic. The acting is pure cheese, and the songs are god-awful, but I could easily watch it every day.

2. *Who's Afraid of Virginia Woolf?* (1966)

I think about Edward Albee's vituperative play about marital warfare every time I go to a really tense dinner party.

3. *Elizabeth* (1998)

This brimming goblet of religious tension, political conspiracy, sex, violence, and war is heaven, thanks to Cate Blanchett's performance as the naïve and vibrant princess who becomes the stubborn and knowing queen. The cold, dark sets paired with the lush costuming show the golden age of England's monarchy emerging from the Middle Ages.

4. *The Queen* (2006)

Yes, I have a crush on Helen Mirren. She does an amazing job in this film, making Queen Elizabeth II (as I mentioned, a dead ringer for my mother!) seem downright human.

5. *Keeper of the Flame* (1942)

Katharine Hepburn plays a national hero's widow. She has a great big secret that's brought out by interviews with a biographer (Spencer Tracy). This is one of my favorite wartime movies.

While we're at it, here are a few more movies that I find inspiring: *The Draughtsman's Contract*, *The Go-Between*, *Prospero's Books*, *Ryan's Daughter*, *Two for the Road*, *Women in Love*, *Waterloo Bridge* (1940), *Portrait of Jennie*, *Elephant Walk*, *How to Marry a Millionaire*, *The Philadelphia Story*, *Darling* (1965), *Meet Me in St. Louis*, *Pee-wee's Big Adventure*, *Bedazzled* (1967), all the James Bond movies, *The Thomas Crown Affair* (1968 and 1999), *The Wizard of Oz*, *My Fair Lady*, *Hannah and Her Sisters*, *Annie Hall*, *Doctor Zhivago*, *Lawrence of Arabia*, *Nicholas and Alexandria*, *War and Peace* (1956), *Giant*, *Gone with the Wind*, *L'avventura*, *Mon Oncle Antoine*, *Zabriskie Point*, *Black Orpheus* (1959), *Orpheus* (1949), and Jean Cocteau's *Beauty and the Beast*.

Any one of these films could inspire a dozen collections.

I also love the worlds created by the writers Thomas Mann, James Agee, Herman Melville, T. S. Eliot, Edna St. Vincent Millay, Sir Arthur Conan Doyle, E. F. Benson, Carson McCullers, and Gertrude Stein, to name a tiny fraction of the authors on my bookshelf.

You can see why I was mad at my students who told me they couldn't find inspiration! I don't care if your list leans away from campy cult classics and period dramas and toward, say, zombie movies or bromances or video games. Any genre, any film, any book can be the jumping-off point for amazing creative work. As long as we have Netflix, Turner Classic Movies, Amazon, YouTube, and bookstores, there is no excuse ever to lack inspiration.

Never Underestimate Karma

BEING NICE TO WAITERS may well be the most important etiquette rule there is. I know a high-ranking executive who is sure to take every potential hire out for a meal, simply because you learn so much about people by how they behave in a restaurant. It's a really good idea whether you're interviewing job candidates or getting to know someone on a first date. So much is revealed.

Case in point: Recently I went out for lunch with some colleagues I'd known for years and thought were lovely people. Suddenly, we're sitting at a restaurant table and they turn into high-maintenance princes and princesses who every five seconds all but snapped their fingers and rolled their eyes in the direction of our perfectly capable servers. I was shocked by how rude they were to the waitstaff. I had to reevaluate them totally. And goodness knows that's the last time I'll invite them out.

One woman I knew would avoid eye contact with the waitress, then mutter and mumble her order. It seemed so hostile. What is that about? Is it a power trip? I feel that whenever people are rude to those whom they feel are beneath them, it is so indicative of character. It's also such hubris. When you see someone who is doing a job you wouldn't want to do, you should simply think: *There but for the grace of God go I.*

Another coworker was particularly horrid on the first and last occasion I ate out with him. He saw waiters as his prey. When they came over to take his order in the middle of a conversation (which, let's face it, is typically most of the time unless you're giving your companion the silent treatment), he had this habit of hissing at them, "I'm speaking."

Can you believe it? I wanted to hide under the table. Now if I need to meet with him, we do so in my office. And how could I ever recommend him for a job or anything else where he'd be dealing with other people? Who knows when this horrid "I'm-speaking" monster would emerge.

Once I learned that some friends were bad tippers, I made sure always to take the bill when dining with them. Then they would admonish me for overtipping. I would say, "It's none of your business how much I tip."

Of course, I don't feel that way when the situation is reversed. When I notice someone I'm eating with is undertipping, I try to throw down an extra bill or two to make it right. But you have to be really sure they don't catch you doing it, because it insults their (albeit totally wrong) sense of themselves as good hosts. Also, it often means you have to have a conversation about whether or not the waiters deserve that extra bill right in front of the waiters, which makes the whole exchange doubly rude.

Now to get to the karma thing: You make yourself so vulnerable by not tipping well or treating people in the service industry with respect. Not only is it wrong to treat another human being like that, but there's a practical consideration: They're standing between you and *eating*. Without waiters, nothing comes to your table, and nothing goes away. Aren't you worried that they'll put rat poison in your food, or at least spit in it? If I were a waiter and someone talked rudely to me, I know I would be seriously tempted. I would never intentionally put someone's life at risk, but half-a-dozen laxative tablets dissolved in a cup of coffee would be very sweet payback, indeed.

When I watch British period movies (*Gosford Park*, for example), I'm struck by how people in service are ignored to the point of invisibility. Is that what this mistreatment of waiters is about? Some kind of reverence for Mother England? We're supposed to be a democracy in this country. We're not supposed to have royalty. From my perspective, getting high and mighty with anyone standing behind a counter or working at a restaurant is downright un-American.

Yes, there are bad waiters. Once at dinner with my family, we had a waitperson drop an entire tray of Bloody Marys on us. My sister had on a white sweater. Her four- and one-year-olds were very upset by the noise and mess and the sudden sight of their mother covered in what looked to them like blood. The whole restaurant stopped and stared at us. And would you believe the waiter and manager didn't even acknowledge it? They didn't give us a discount on our bill, nor did they apologize. That's the rare situation when I think it's fair to tip less than the going rate.

My niece, Wallace, was in town recently, and we went out for dinner. She's doing some teaching and loves it. We were chatting away about academia. The restaurant was crowded, so we ate at the bar. The bartender was incredibly nice, so we talked with him a bit. At the end of the night he comped our drinks because he said, "You were so nice!"

I thought about it, and we hadn't been *that* nice. We'd just been friendly and polite. I guess that's rare enough to make him impressed. How disappointing is that?

Now that I think about it, when faced with unexpected generosity, I'm always floored. Once I was having lunch at Michael's with Grace Mirabella when a man came up and introduced himself as Mickey Drexler. Mickey was the CEO of the Gap for many years and had just moved over to J. Crew. He said he was a big fan of the show.

"Well, I'm a big fan of what you did with the Gap," I said, "and I can't wait to see what you do at J. Crew." (As we know now, he did an amazing job repositioning that brand.)

The next day, I received a handwritten card from Mickey Drexler with a 30 percent off J. Crew Friends and Family discount card *for life*.

I GO FOR LONG periods of time when I feel like casual politeness is completely extinct. I received an e-mail recently from a certain glamorous host of *Top Chef*. I won't say who she is, but she was once married to a world-famous novelist who received death threats.

She told me she was looking for a jewelry designer for her line, and I said I would put my radar up and send her anyone I found who might be a good fit. Well, I found someone terrific, discovered she was available, and sent along her résumé. I was very proud of myself for making such a great match.

Then I never heard back. Nor did the designer. I was so embarrassed. Here I had this great jewelry designer all excited, and then it was as if I'd made up the whole gig. Either the glamorous host should have followed up with the designer about the project or written one of us back to say, "I found someone, but thank you so much."

Without that acknowledgment, I have to assume she didn't really want my help after all, so I'll keep that in mind if she ever asks for anything again.

To be honest, few people will help you a first time, especially in fashion. This business is so ruthless. I hope I'm not destroying anyone's warm and fuzzy feelings about the industry to reveal this, but many fashion designers really and truly hate one another. I think it's because there is only a finite number of people who buy very expensive clothes, so the thinking among designers is: "They have my customer" or "That order could be mine if they weren't here."

Of course, plenty of people in the fashion world are wonderful. When John Bartlett, a lovely man, closed his Claiborne by John Bartlett brand, there were people saying, "It's because he's too nice that this happened to him."

No! It's the economy, among other things. The only difference between him and all the horrible divas who lost their jobs at the same time is that now everyone wants to work with John because he's such a great guy, and no one wants to work with the others.

Certain awful people prosper in the short term, but how much fun is your life if you're a diva everyone hates? And if bad behavior happens at the office, it almost always happens at home, too. People make excuses for divas. I don't want an excuse. I don't care about the reasons behind extreme misbehavior. I don't want to sound coldhearted, but it makes me crazy when people say, "Well, X is happening to her, so of course she's yelling at her assistant." If X is happening to you, that should be all the more reason to keep everyone close by being kind.

To his immense credit, Michael Kors is a diplomat who takes the high road. But most designers are totally threatened by other designers. When we have two designer guest judges, you can feel the hostility in the studio. The judging is edited in such a way that you usually can't tell, but every now and then you'll catch a whiff of the tension. Multiply that bitchy glance by a million, and you'll get some sense of what it's like.

I'm reminded of that scene in the fashion documentary *Valentino: The Last Emperor* in which Karl Lagerfeld takes Valentino aside at Valentino's party and tells him they're the only two good designers in the world—which I take to mean, "I am the only good designer. Look what a good guest I'm being! I'm calling you a peer!"

European designers in particular hate American ones. They see Americans as sellouts and too commercial. This may just be my patriotism speaking (and I do love my country), but from my point of view, our hypercommercialism and obsession with pop culture actually make American clothes great.

There's something very outdated about the European way of talking about these things. If you look at what walks down the couture runways in Paris, it's not what the customers actually buy. People used to. In the sixties and even into the seventies, women of a certain social station would actually buy couture. And it used to be that couture week had a dramatic impact on the world. There was a trickle-down effect.

But now? There used to be more than two hundred couture houses in Paris. Now there are, what, a dozen? And Lindsay Lohan is designing for one of them!

There's a quote from me floating around about this. A *New York* magazine reporter asked me at a party how I felt about Lindsay Lohan designing for Emanuel Ungaro. I was taken aback because I hadn't heard anything about it until then. I said that if it was true, "It's got to be a publicity stunt. Or a crack-smoking board of directors?"

How I said it was a little blunt, but I stand by the sentiment. I mean, Lindsay Lohan knows how to buy things, but does she know how to design? And if she does, then at that level?

The critics didn't think so. Her eighties-inspired debut in the fall 2009 collection was panned. *Women's Wear Daily,* the fashion-world bible, called it "an embarrassment."

Well, at least Ungaro is trying new things and attempting to stay modern. Christian Lacroix has been having big trouble because he has only the couture line and has long seemed averse to any kind of modernization. There was talk about having the French government bail out the company—after more than two decades of losses. If I were a French citizen, I'd question whether that was a wise investment of tax money.

Fashion designers aren't the only people who resent other people in their own industry. You also see massive contempt among peers in architecture.

I learned a fair amount about architecture when I was associate dean of Parsons and was charged with restoring the school's defunct Interior Design Department. It had a rich history at the college, but in the sixties a decision was made to close it down. The belief at the time was that, given all the upheaval in the country—the assassination of President Kennedy, difficulties in Cuba, the brewing war in Vietnam—it wasn't socially responsible to teach students how to design apartments for the rich.

Well, given that interior design was the largest academic program at the school at that time, the enrollment in the whole school collapsed, the Board of Trustees resigned en masse, and ultimately, owing to a financial crisis, it had to combine with the New School for Social Research.

To bring back the program, I met with countless people in the industry, including members of venerable old firms. Most of the famous designers I spoke with were known for classic, traditional interiors. Their clients have antiques and Old Master paintings and zillions of dollars with which to outfit their apartments on Fifth Avenue. And even though these high-end designers have a lot in common, they talk trash about one another to no end.

I mentioned one popular name to another well-known designer, and she flew into a rage: "He thinks he can put a glass coffee table in the middle of a traditional room and call it something special! I can use a glass coffee table, too!"

I found it scary how incensed these well-heeled people could get about a coffee table.

Architects are even worse! They tend to look down on interior designers. One architect I know said, "Interior designers are to architects as flight attendants are to pilots." By contrast, interior designers often decry architects, because much of a designer's job is fixing mistakes made by architects. We all have odd architectural features in our homes, like the closet door you can't open if the front door is open. Interior designers pride themselves on coming up with clever fixes for such awkward corners.

At the Council of Fashion Designers of America dinners, it's a big huggy, kissy meet and greet, but make no mistake: these people are cutthroat. Even the supportive Michael Kors loves to read the bad reviews in *Women's Wear Daily* out loud to entertain us on set. I couldn't help but notice when he had less-than-stellar reviews one year he skipped that issue.

The upside is that this level of jealousy helps make the industry more competitive, which I believe is ultimately good for the quality of work that's produced. You do need to be careful, though, if you present any kind of threat to a fashion or interior designer or an architect. Don't go down a dark alley with anyone in the design world who might envy you.

Niceties Are Nice

IS CHIVALRY DEAD? I hope not, but I am always discouraged when I hear people complain about "old-fashioned" acts of politeness. For example, I have heard women complain about men holding doors for them, as if it is inherently offensive and implies that they are weak.

How outrageous is that? I hold doors for women, and I also hold them for men. When I'm at Macy's, I don't let the door slam behind me when I walk through. It has nothing to do with gender. I would hold a door for anyone.

Would I hold the door for a dog? Okay, maybe not, because a dog shouldn't be at Macy's, but otherwise, yes! It has to do with noticing our fellow human beings and saying, "I recognize that you're on this planet, and I don't want a door hitting you in the face."

That said, I did once have a terrible door-holding experience at D'Agostino's supermarket in the Upper East Side's Yorkville area, where I lived for seven years. This little old lady was trying to leave the store and was having the hardest time with the door. She kept pushing, pushing, pushing. To help her out, I pushed the door open for her. Well, she fell flat on her face on the pavement. We had to call an ambulance. I thought, *That's where politeness will get you; I caused this by trying to help.* It was horrible. I try to do a nice thing for her . . . and I end up putting her in the hospital.

I learned a lesson from that. It's important not to be over-zealous in helping. Since then, faced with a similar situation, I broach the topic first. I say, "May I help you?" Then, assuming the little old lady says yes, I push the door open. To date, I am proud to say, I haven't put any more senior citizens in the ER.

If I've made errors of overaction, at least I am not guilty of letting opportunities to be decent pass by. Honestly, I don't understand how people can navigate the world and pretend no one else exists, like people who have big backpacks and yet barrel through narrow aisles. I don't mind if people have huge bags, but what's wrong with "Excuse me"? Why don't they take the bag off their shoulder when they're on the subway and put it on the floor?

Treating others nicely is such an easy thing to do, and it makes other people so happy. You'll see people's eyes light up—mine, at least—when someone smiles and says a genuine thank-you to a Starbucks barista, or asks, "Is this bag in your way?" when they have a huge suitcase on public transporta-tion.

The other day at the grocery store, I needed a lemon, and there was no way to get to it through the throng of shopping carts, so I did my other shopping in the store and then came back. Instantly, other shoppers who were picking up fruit boxed me in with their carts. I thought: *I'm not in a hurry. I can wait for these carts to move.*

So I waited patiently for the carts to part. I waited . . . and waited. I was clearly there waiting, but the woman next to me just didn't move. When I finally asked her, "Could you please move so I might get out?" she glared at me with a look of annoyance, as if I were ruining her shopping trip.

I thought: *It's a good thing I'm not an axe murderer.*

Really, people who act like they're the only ones on the planet are taking their lives in their hands each and every day. What if the person they wall in at the grocery store or bump with their backpack on the bus isn't a mild-mannered pacifist like me? You hear all the time about road rage landing people in the hospital. Bad behavior isn't only rude—it's also dangerous.

YOU HAVE PRECIOUS FEW moments to make a first impression. It must be positive. One can lose out so quickly by not making eye contact, not emoting, not having a firm handshake, or not shaking hands at all.

Whatever the outcome of the meeting, at least you can say, "I did my best. I pulled off my end of this thing."

There is no excuse not to reply when someone speaks to you. I say "Good morning" to the doorman in our building every day, and he never even looks up. If I ask him a question, he mumbles unintelligibly. I see him on the sidewalk talking to friends, engaged in an animated conversation, so I know he's capable of talking. He just seems to be completely withdrawn around people he doesn't know well.

I hear this a lot as an excuse for why people don't take chances or don't succeed in getting the job they want or the relationship they desire: "I'm so shy. I get very nervous."

"I'm shy by nature!" I say. "I'm withdrawn. You have to learn how to engage. If I did, anyone can."

Remember, I was so scared before my first day of teaching that I threw up! I still went into that classroom. And if I hadn't, I probably wouldn't be writing this book now.

IF THERE'S ONE SITUATION in which good behavior should be easy, it's following the birth of a child. New babies are typically the source of extreme happiness all around, so I'm always shocked when people behave badly toward new parents. The appropriate thing to do is to send a note of congratulations, in which you offer to help in any way you can, and ideally a small gift for the child as well. And yet, my friends with young children say it is rare that people follow this protocol. With couples unsuccessfully trying to conceive I can speculate that there could be a jealousy among some friends, but they're the only ones whose reluctance to celebrate makes sense to me.

Also, for friends who are a bit immature, maybe the baby poses a threat. Having that baby means the parents are really cemented to their nuclear family. Friends whom the couple has coddled may think, *You can't have a baby! I'm your baby!*

But no matter what qualms you might have, it's important to suck it up and send that note of congratulations. New parents often feel very alone and very tired. They need a little cheerleading from the people who love them.

So how about visiting? If you're lucky enough to be invited to see a new baby, be sure to bring food for the sleepy new parents, and don't stay long. Also, do whatever you're asked. For example, germs can be very scary for new parents, and you may be asked to wash your hands before holding the baby.

Aunts and grandmothers often think, *Wash what? Give me that baby!* Just do whatever will make the parents most comfortable, even if that means scrubbing down as if you're preparing for surgery.

The parents can facilitate this, though. What about walking around with wet wipes? You're making good hygiene easy. It's not a blockade around the baby, but it's a moat. Antibacterial wipes are the drawbridge, as in: "Would you like to hold the baby? Yes? Great! Have a Wet One!"

Breast-feeding in public is a really hot topic right now. On one hand, you have activists who say you should never cover up, ever—nurse loud, nurse proud! Others say you should never leave the house—and, by the way, keep the blinds down!

I was breast-fed. My younger sister, Kim, was not. Between 1953 and 1956, the pediatrician went from encouraging breast-feeding to saying, "We don't do this anymore." And now, of course, it's back in vogue. It seems to me that there are ways of nursing comfortably and whenever necessary while still staying fairly discreet. As long as we're encouraging women to breast-feed, we should make sure we support them in the practice.

I once had a coworker who was pumping all the time. Often I wished she had the baby with her. I know she and the baby missed each other, and from my perspective babies are a lot more fun to have around than machinery. Workplaces seem to be evolving in such a way that families are taken into account more, and I think that's certainly the future.

NOW LET'S TALK ABOUT the manners around one of the most enjoyable social graces: gift giving. Giving gifts is so much fun.

There's a thrill in choosing an item you think someone will enjoy. A lot of work goes into getting and sending a present. There's the cost of the gift, sure, but also the wrapping, the ribbon, the card, and the horrible line at the post office.

My niece, Wallace, and I tried to convince everyone in our family to do Secret Santa or some other gift-giving game that would allow us to buy only one or two presents rather than the dozens the family now seems to expect.

"I like getting lots of presents for people," my mother said. "I'm an old lady. I can do whatever I want!"

"Okay," Wallace said, "then how about a theme? Like next year the gift theme could be *cheese*. It doesn't have to be a big hunk of Edam. It could be *cheesy*, like *Valley of the Dolls*." Wallace and I were thrilled with ourselves for having come up with that.

The family didn't go for that, either.

I forget how sensitive people are on the subject of presents. I joked on a Lifetime holiday promo about how homemade gifts say "love" and also say "cheapskate."

Well, there was an outcry on the message boards over that. One person wrote, "Your commercial in affect [*sic*] was insulting and DEMEANING to those of us who hold the welfare of our loved ones above the commercialism of the season."

I received a similarly angry letter from a viewer about how, because of hard times, the family was making fudge for presents rather than shopping. She felt I'd belittled that choice.

I felt horrible. I wrote the letter writer a note apologizing for having been so flippant. And I really did feel sorry. But I also thought, *It was a joke*. And I think people should own their situation, whatever it is. There's no shame in being a cheapskate when you're poor. I think she could have written a note with her gift saying, "Fudge says love, and it says we're broke. Here you go. Love you!" I would love to get fudge, especially with a cute note like that.

Anyway, whether you get or make a present for someone, you want to have the gift appreciated, or at least acknowledged. When there is no reaction—no thank-you card, no e-mail, no phone call—you start to wonder whether it even arrived. It's like throwing gifts into a big black hole.

I have a friend who sends her nieces and nephews gifts every year for Christmas and then hears . . . nothing. No note, no call—not from them, not from their parents.

My advice? Cut them off. If people don't even acknowledge your gifts, you have to assume they don't like them and don't want any more. When people don't communicate with you, you can only go by their actions, and if their actions are to give no indication that they want you to keep doing what you're doing, you might as well stop.

When Christmas morning arrives and they look for that box among the piles, maybe they'll realize that their silence has had an effect. How great would it be to be a fly on the wall in that house?

"Where is it?" you can imagine them asking.

Where is it? You never noticed when it came—how it is you notice when it doesn't?

My mother reached that point with a relative. She never heard a word after the gifts stopped, and she was sorry she hadn't stopped sooner.

At the same time, giving people something you know they're going to love is thrilling, and when it's acknowledged it makes you closer to that person. Thank-you cards are an opportunity to tell the giver how happy you are to be considered, and to tell them how much they mean to you. It's a lovely part of social life.

Alas, I am afraid the thank-you note and even the ritual of gift giving are on the outs these days. I've heard of these things called "no-gift parties"—wedding invitations that say things like "No presents, please," or funerals that request that mourners donate to a charity instead of sending flowers.

I'm just baffled. Why would you want to derail people who have a good impulse? Don't people who are getting married need things? Charity should be part of the whole year. Everyone should give back. But weddings, like birthdays, should be a really special occasion. If there are no presents, why bother having a party? You can see your friends anytime.

Children especially need to receive presents. Not only do they want them—and why shouldn't they—but presents are good for them. When they open presents in front of people, they learn how to be gracious, even when they get something they don't want or when they get two of the same thing. (Not that there's much chance of that these days—there are so many different kinds of toys now. I was looking at the Toys "R" Us catalogue. There were four pages of Legos. My inner child almost fainted.)

All that said, I have to tell you a secret: I am the worst gift recipient in the world. I have a closet full of unopened gifts. I'm in denial about them. I should probably seek therapy for it. I love showering other people with gifts, but I don't want to get them.

To clarify: With people I know, I'm pretty good with thank-yous. It's when strangers send me things that I freeze up. The obligation such gifts raise in me outweighs the joy they provide.

So to all the strangers who have sent me gifts: a great, belated thanks to you all, and I'm sorry I was too overwhelmed to respond before now. I love whatever it is, and it was so generous and sweet of you to think of me. Now please take anything else you might want to send and give it to someone more deserving.

Why, you may ask, don't I just pass along all those unwanted gifts to others who may enjoy them? Well, I learned the hard way that regifting is dangerous. When I was at Parsons, there was a going-away party for a coworker I had been extremely fond of at one time but then came not to like very much. I was planning to sit out the farewell fete, but some colleagues insisted I go. I was very reluctant but finally agreed, and I thought I would just go to my gift closet and find something appropriate to bring her.

I found a silver Tiffany pen. It seemed perfect: not too personal, but nice. I'd been given it when I judged an art contest among the employees of the Port Authority. It had been a great event on the sixtieth floor of the North Tower of the World Trade Center, a long time ago.

At the party, I presented her with that beautiful little blue box with the white ribbon, and she was delighted. She opened the box and pulled out the pen with a smile on her face. Then she said, "Oh, look, and it's engraved, too!" As she read the engraving, her face fell: "Best wishes from the Port Authority of New York and New Jersey."

It was very embarrassing. And yet, once the first flush of shame had passed, I thought it was pretty appropriate. I didn't want to go to the party. I didn't want to bring her anything. And so even though I went, my true feelings crept through. In effect, my elegant Tiffany pen bitch-slapped her. That's a situation where I should have just trusted my instincts and stayed home.

I've been on the other side of this kind of faux pas, too. When I was living on Perry Street in the West Village, there was—and I believe still is—an annual street fair called the Perry-phernalia Block Party. My neighbors Bea and Jerry Banu and I always sat together out on the stoop. In fact, Jerry was in charge of the event. One year, as my dear friend Bea was setting up her table she declared, "I'm going to get all the jewelry I don't like," and she came back out with a box full of things I had given her!

"I'm glad to know you don't like this stuff!" I said. "Now I can stop giving it to you!" She was mortified, but I said, "Don't bring it back inside. It's done. Forget about it. Maybe now they can find a happy home." It's good that I don't have an ego about these things.

And I was serious about being glad to know. I know it's not proper to tell people when they have terrible taste or to specify what you'd like for the holidays, but sometimes I wish I could.

My mother to this day buys me socks and underwear—and in the wrong size, no less! I am fifty-seven years old, and she still buys me things in a size L—large. No matter how many times I tell her, "Mother, I'm a medium. I always have been!" she doesn't listen. And every year I have to return what she gets me.

One time she bought me a shirt that came in a Lord & Taylor box. I went to the Men's Department to exchange it for another size, and they said they didn't carry the item at all. I called my mother to tell her, and she gasped. "I got it at an outlet," she said, blushing through the phone. "I just used the Lord and Taylor box."

When pressed on her dubiously successful gift giving, my mother just gets defensive. "You and your sister and your niece and nephew are so hard to buy for," she told me recently, "because you have no interests."

"What? No interests? Wait a minute!" I said. "Just to speak for myself, I am passionate about many, many things. I love fashion. I love design. I love books. I love architecture. I love movies. I could go on! You could get me any book. You could get me a DVD. An Amazon gift card."

For me, gift cards are fantastic. Whenever I don't have a perfect, one-of-a-kind gift in mind for someone, I love to give gift cards. Alas, my family says that's too impersonal. They're always complaining when I give these cards, saying I didn't take the time to find the perfect gift for each person. I finally told my sister, "Apparently, my hinting has been too subtle. I get these for people because I'd like to *receive* them."

And they're way better than crazy objects that I then have to move around my house and hide in closets. Recently, I was given an objet d'art by some friends. They have never been in my apartment, and when I saw what they sent, quite frankly I was insulted. It's grotesque, and 100 percent not me. I wish I could show it to you so you could see how there is no apartment on the planet, at least none I'd want to visit, where this could possibly look good. It's ambitiously bad.

Why did these friends feel I needed that piece of bizarre sculpture in my life? I was honored that they wanted to give me something, but it's very presumptuous to get people things that are going to take up a lot of space in their lives unless you know for a fact that they will really love it.

That's why I find registries very handy. You can see what people need and want and what other people have already bought for them. It takes all the pressure off and makes you feel like you're getting something that's really going to be appreciated.

I've bought a lot of presents off gift registries, but truth be told, I haven't been to a wedding in fourteen years. I'm old enough that, by now, people in my peer group have either married or they haven't. And if they're doing it for a second time, it's usually a small event with just a few family members, so I just send a small gift to acknowledge the event.

The last wedding I went to was at the couple's house in Greenwich, Connecticut. They were fashion people. They had a big tent in the backyard and every possible bell and whistle. There were probably 350 or 400 guests. Even the Porta-Potties were fully equipped, luxurious trailers. I was sitting at the table of the grandmother of the bride, and I said to her, looking around in awe, "This is phenomenal!"

She looked at me with a trace of pity and said, "You must not get out much."

This was the bride's grandmother! Isn't she supposed to rave about her family? Isn't she supposed to be enthusiastic?

She's right, I don't get out much, I thought. *But even so! This is an incredible wedding.*

This couple really wanted a lavish party, but I pity brides today who feel that breaking the bank is an obligation. Weddings seem so stressful to me in general; it's a wonder how anyone who's throwing one feels like getting married at all by the end.

I know someone who rented the whole Yale Club and had a towering raw bar for the postceremony cocktail hour. This was before the multicourse sit-down dinner for more than two hundred people. They must have spent a quarter of a million dollars.

I always say in a case where you're already breaking the bank (as on one of those ridiculously priced designer handbags), you should spend 10 percent less than you've budgeted and give that extra money to charity. Your wedding guests won't notice if there's one less tier of oysters and lobster claws, but 10 percent of a fortune can make a real difference to people who truly need it.

Given how expensive weddings can be these days, I understand how eager the couple is to receive money as a gift, but if that's the case, they should simply throw a cheaper party. I have thankfully never been to a wedding where the bride walks around with a money bag, though I have heard tell of them. Miss Manners calls this "simple social blackmail," and she's right.

Besides, there's no shame in marrying simply. In Washington when I was growing up, weddings were typically a ceremony followed by a champagne reception. There was never a meal associated with a wedding. If you felt you had to feed the out-of-town people, you did it the night before at the rehearsal dinner. Ultimately, whenever you're entertaining, it's good to work within the budget you have, and if that means you just do a cocktail hour, that's totally fine. Just make sure it's a fun and gracious cocktail hour.

Generally speaking, I am all for doing things cheaply whenever possible. For example, I prefer not to take taxis or limos. For some reason, people don't believe that I take public transportation. They assume that I have a car service, or maybe even a sedan chair carried by nubile models. In fact, I take the subway twice a day on average, and I salute its relative speed and convenience.

The subway is, however, a petri dish of bad manners. I'm not talking about mild nuances of behavior or even some of the craziness that takes place within the train's cars or on the more oppressive platforms where riders sweat or freeze and hold their nose or ears. That's just the sound and smell of New York.

I'm talking about the way people push and shove and act as if they are in the Thunderdome. Why do people ascending the stairs behave as though it's perfectly acceptable to leave no room for people who are descending and vice versa? There is adequate room for one aisle to go up and one to go down.

What happened to using words instead of actions as the means of moving past people who are obstacles in your path? I find that merely saying, "Excuse me, please . . ." is a successful method. I have never needed to push, shove, or body block my way through a crowd, so you needn't, either. And remember that backpacks, wheeled luggage, and baby strollers were not invented to be used as battering rams. I like getting around the city fast, but I often feel kind of beaten up by the time I reach my destination.

Another place where it seems like niceties have been completely abandoned is on airplanes. I have to fly all the time for work. As we know, flying used to be a very glamorous thing and is now only a hair less miserable than a cross-country trip on an un-air-conditioned bus in August.

Still, quite frankly, I look forward to that airline door closing. There is no phone. There is no Internet (although airborne Internet access is surely in our future). I am insulated. I can actually just focus and write on my computer or read a book. It's heaven. But I can't sleep on planes, which is why taking overnight flights makes me crazy. I am always wide awake. I am the perfect person for the exit row. If the pilot ever needs me, I am right there, ready to go.

Maybe that's why strange things are always happening to me on planes. One time, I had my seat in coach and was just about to start reading when a woman came down the aisle with an eight- or nine-year-old child and sat next to me in the middle seat, with this large child on her lap. She thought children could travel for free, and no one had stopped her.

Seats today are close quarters to begin with, but this was ridiculous. No one in the aisle could move. Eventually, the flight attendant came and sorted things out and explained that children over two need their own seats, but until then I thought I was going to be pinned down by a large preteen for the whole flight.

Once when I flew from Paris to New York, we made an emergency landing in Boston because a famous nightclub owner and her teenage son refused to stop smoking. Something similar happened once when I was flying from New York to Detroit early on a Sunday morning. There was a bad-tuxedo group—the men wearing these hideous purple and pale blue tuxedos and the women clad in acetate gowns—throwing lit cigarettes at one another. The pilot ended up leaving the cockpit to come yell at them. When we landed, the sheriff got on board and took them away.

Another time when I boarded, an older man was sitting in my seat. I asked him about his seat, and he didn't seem to understand me. I said, "If you're in my seat, where's your seat? Because I'll sit in it."

When that failed, I approached the flight attendant and explained the situation. She said, "Well, just take a seat."

"Aren't these seats assigned?" I asked.

"Yes," she said, "but if someone comes and you're in his seat, you can just move."

"But this man in my seat must have an assignment of his own." I said again. "Can't you just help me figure out what it is, and then I'll sit there? It will make it so much easier for everyone."

She was completely and totally uninterested in helping facilitate. I realized I was being really annoying, but I stood in the vestibule by the entrance to the plane until there was only one seat left, and then I sat there.

So it's not just the fellow passengers who can make a flight difficult, sometimes it's the flight attendants. They say they're there for your safety and to do anything they can to make you more comfortable, but sometimes their stress levels get the better of them and they become more like jail wardens than attendants.

On a flight to Tampa for a speaking assignment, I sensed there was going to be trouble when I saw a very young flight attendant who seemed furious. Can't you just tell when someone has an aura of hostility? The second you see them you know they're going to be troublesome. Sure enough, a woman came on the plane with a huge, unwieldy roller bag, and she told this angry flight attendant, "Excuse me, but I'm going to need help putting this in the overhead."

The response: "Then you had no business bringing it on board."

Debatable.

"But I do have it on board," the woman said, "and I do need help."

And the flight attendant said, "Well, you're not getting any help from me. That's not what we're here for. When you get to your seat, you'll have to ask someone."

"And if they won't help me?"

"We'll have to check it."

She had a curtness and a dismissiveness that I found very unpleasant.

And she later did something even worse. During the safety demonstration, she was pantomiming along to the safety instructional. I was reading a book. Others were engaged in their own work. Suddenly, she stopped what she was doing, paused the recording, and, with her two-inch-heeled foot, kicked the newspaper of the person in the first row! She shouted, "I'm not doing this demonstration to entertain myself!"

Frankly, I worried about her blood pressure.

Carrying around anger like that is really dangerous, but I think it's up to each of us to deal with it on our own time. I hate confrontation and am so turned off by people who insist on starting fights all the time. Some people are so insecure that they will push a confrontation at every opportunity. There are even people who at a party (often after a few glasses of something) will blurt out things to others like, "I feel like you don't like me."

It's so childish, and it never ends well. Either they say that, actually, they don't like you, and then there's awkwardness. Or they say they do like you, but you've just put them in an uncomfortable position, so you'll never know if you just coerced that answer—or if at that moment, because of the question, they actually stopped liking you.

Remember at the playground when kids would ask each other a million times, "Are you my best friend?"

After the tenth time you want to say, "Well, not anymore!"

I still remember the grade-school drama involving my oldest friend, Doug Harbison, and my new friend, Craig Smith. I felt confident enough about Doug's friendship that I could assure Craig that he was my best friend because I thought nothing would alienate Doug. I was wrong. It really hurt Doug's feelings, and I felt terrible.

Bad manners often come from a place of deep unhappiness. It's almost a declaration of bad citizenship, a way of challenging the world: "Why should I be a good citizen? You haven't been good to me!"

Frankly, in my experience, people who try to put you on the spot about your feelings are just angry with you, and they're projecting negative feelings onto you. They want to start a fight so they have an excuse to be so upset. Often the anger is based on your aloofness. They're thinking, *Where does he get off not liking me? I'm very likable!*

You know, this book started out as an etiquette book, but at times I've thought, *Maybe it's too tough to behave well under all the crazy circumstances modern life throws at you.*

Do you know how Amy Vanderbilt, the etiquette maven, died? In 1974, she fell or jumped out of the second-story window of her East Eighty-seventh Street town house. It was mysterious. I wonder sometimes if the number of things that could go wrong between people just overwhelmed her and she lost all interest in avoiding pitfalls like open windows.

In fact, when you start thinking about how cruel people can be to one another, you wonder whether you should become an advocate not for manners but for living in a cave with a boulder rolled in front of it. Life is full of many shocking surprises and upsetting interactions. Maybe we should all opt out.

Especially because becoming a hermit brings up some

great design opportunities. We can bring back the fifties bomb shelter.

My mother was very into that idea back in the day. She was looking at plans right and left and stocking up for it. I think I was in my twenties when she finally got rid of all the boxes with the gallon plastic containers of distilled water and the by-then-exploded canned food.

I didn't care about preparing for the apocalypse, but I did love the architecture. The shelter was basically a submarine with a big periscope. The thought of a nuclear war terrified me, and I didn't enjoy the nuclear drills we had to do at my school. I used to think, *I don't think hiding under our desks is a useful exercise. Will it really protect us if bombs fall and the whole building caves in?* I was a critic even then.

Ultimately, though, I think leaving your subbasement is well worth the trouble. And what else can we do? We're human beings. Try as we might to avoid it, and as hard as it might sometimes be to act civil, the truth is this: We need one another.

Physical Comfort Is Overrated

WHENEVER I MEET NEW people, almost without fail they say, "I was so afraid of what you'd say about my clothes!" The truth is: I really don't take note of what other people wear unless their outfit blows my mind for good or for ill, and even in that case I will rarely say anything unless I'm asked.

When I was taping *Extra!* the other day, the camera guy said, "Oh God, I just know you're going to be disappointed in what I'm wearing."

"That's ridiculous," I said. "You're hoisting a camera and down on your knees and moving around. You need to be agile. It wouldn't be right for you to be in a tailored suit! You're dressed appropriately!"

I get a little shrill when I talk about it, because it seems like people are either too worried about what they have on or not worried enough. People are really intimidated by fashion, and as an educator and a fashion lover I think that's such a shame.

Meryl Streep said in a 2009 *Vanity Fair* article that she was over trying to appeal to men. "I can't remember the last time I really worried about being appealing," she said.

I don't totally believe that she doesn't care. It is true that she's really eschewed fashion. I think it's smart, intellectual Meryl speaking, saying she's too smart for style. But no one's too smart for it. Providing we leave our cave, it matters to all of us.

When we look good, we feel better. That's true for everyone. You feel better able to tackle the world. It's not a good feeling going into an exam without having prepared, and it's not a good feeling leaving the house without having dressed to be around people. Just the way it never rains when you have an umbrella, you'll never run into people if you look fantastic. But go outside in pajamas, and you'll run into every ex you have.

The key is not being dressy. The key is being appropriate.

Someone at my neighborhood grocery store once said to me, "Wow, you really do wear jeans and a T-shirt!"

"Yes," I said, "at the *grocery store*."

It's all about context. I wear a suit to work, to weddings, to funerals, to the theater, and to church. When shopping at the grocery store or running errands, I have been known to wear jeans, because it's totally appropriate. The jeans fit me and are clean, and I usually pair them with a jacket, but yes, jeans!

Some people think of dressing up or being polite as a burden. They think having to wear a tie or use the right fork or send a thank-you card is a kind of shackle. To these people I say: Getting out of bed is a shackle. If you feel that way, stay in it! Invest in a hospital gurney and wheel yourself around on it when you need to go out.

I get very impatient with this whole "comfort issue" with clothing. Yes, you don't feel as comfortable in clothes that fit you as you do in your pajamas and robe. That's a *good* thing. You're navigating a world where you need to have your wits about you. If you're in a lackadaisical comfort haze, you can't be engaged in the world the way you need to be.

Would I be more comfortable in a business meeting wearing my pajamas?

No! It would feel, honestly, very weird. I would think, *Where's my IV? When do I take my next meds?*

Wanting to look good in public has to do with the respect that I have for myself and the respect that I have for the people around me. One of the things I love about New York City is how much people dress up for one another. Walking down the street is such a pleasure, because people are really turned out. Yes, it probably took them more than five minutes to get ready, but it was so worth it. They make the city a prettier place.

In her wonderful memoir *D.V.*, Diana Vreeland (who was born exactly fifty years to the day before me—lucky me!) talks about how she prepared nightly for the arrival of her husband. She dressed up for him every single night:

> *Isn't it curious that even after more than forty years of marriage, I was always slightly shy of him? I can remember his coming home in the evening—the way the door would close and the sound of his step . . . If I was in my bath or in my bedroom making up, I can remember always pulling myself up, thinking, "I must be at my very best." There was never a time when I didn't have that reaction—ever.*

That's kind of lovely, I think. It's always better to err on the side of beauty over comfort. It might get tiresome in practice, but it's a sweet idea. And it's certainly better than being the dowdy, depressing, slatternly housewife played by Shirley Booth in *Come Back, Little Sheba*.

People who are lazy about grooming make me a little crazy. And I'm not talking about getting a blowout or putting on a ton of makeup or getting a haircut every week. I'm talking about bathing and other basics. What are you saying about yourself and about your feelings for the people around you if you give up on these simple things? You're saying, "I don't care." And if you don't care about yourself or the people around you, why should others care about you?

Grooming inappropriately can be as bad as not doing it at all. One time I was out to brunch, and a patron at the restaurant started clipping his nails. He was even with someone, who you'd think would have stopped him! It's such a distinct noise. My gag reflex kicked in. When you see it on the subway, it's bad enough, but at a restaurant? There was a lot of eye contact around the room, but the staff didn't throw him out. He just finished, and then left the clippings there on the floor for the staff to clean up. That's in my bad behavior hall of fame, and it's a good example of someone being far too comfortable out in public.

I also question people's definition of "comfort." Sure, oversize T-shirts feel soft on your body, but you know what's genuinely comfortable? Being dressed appropriately for your surroundings. It feels good at the end of the day to take off your fancy shoes and put on your slippers, but it also feels good to know that all day you looked good and smelled good and that the people you encountered had a positive impression of you and enjoyed having you around.

For my job with Liz Claiborne Inc., I host a ton of shopping mall events. I'll be honest with you: I love them. My colleague Leah Salak and I do Liz Claiborne Inc. multibrand fashion shows for the shoppers at the mall. We pull clothes from the mall's own stores so the customers can actually buy what they see. It's fun and it's also intended to be educational. We show people how they can mix and match, how they can take a dress from day to night, and how an item of apparel can be made ever more versatile.

We work with five to seven of our brands, which include Lucky Brand Jeans, Kate Spade, Juicy Couture, and DKNY Jeans. I always mix them up as much as possible. The business-side people always complain about mixing and matching on the runway. For them, taking a Kate Spade dress and putting a Juicy Couture coat over it is some kind of sacrilege. But I'm very blunt: People don't wear one designer head to toe. So we show people how they actually will wear things, and ultimately, I think it benefits all the brands, because you see how versatile each item is.

Then we have a Q&A session after, and I always find it so touching how women will stand up in front of eight hundred to a thousand people, open up their jackets, and say, "Tim, look how thick I am through here. How can my clothing help me with this?"

It's so wonderful how comfortable they are talking to me about these things. I love hearing about real people with real issues. We live in a bubble here in New York. Of course, I mostly like the bubble! But I also like to get out of it for a reality check, and the reality is that a lot of people are not comfortable with their bodies and need a little help making what they have work for them.

Maybe it will be helpful to hear that even in New York, the women who are supposed to be fashion idols aren't happy with their bodies. When I've gone to the *Vogue* offices I'm always struck by how insanely thin everyone is, even the editorial assistants, who aren't in front of a camera. I think: *How many eating disorders are there on this floor?*

One former editorial assistant I know says that even though she's a healthy weight and height and usually wears a size 8 or 10, she felt morbidly obese while she was working there.

Isn't that a sick statement on the industry?

There is a famous cafeteria in the Condé Nast Building, which houses *Vogue, The New Yorker, Glamour,* and a ton of other magazines. It's a feat of architecture, and yet everything about it horrifies me. Everyone there is so thin, and no one is eating the gourmet food on her plate. There are skinny mirrors on your way out. You know, throwing up your food is not healthy, just as obesity isn't healthy.

I'm always saying I have the greatest respect for whatever size a woman is. We can work with whatever we have. To larger women who want to feel good about their bodies, I'm always talking about the opera divas—those big, beautiful, proud women who are so sexy and powerful. It's ridiculous that a woman with that kind of build wouldn't celebrate it. I know I find curves attractive on women, and most of the men I know do, too.

Of course, I also want people to be healthy. The girth issue in America is not about the clothes. You can dress the opera divas, and they can look great. It's about health. I know how hard it is to lose weight when you drive everywhere and fast food is so cheap. For what I pay for a deli wrap sandwich across the street, I could go to McDonald's twice, and that makes a big difference if you don't have a huge food budget. But you have to find a way to stay healthy no matter what your budget is, whether that means exercise or cooking fresh food.

If a very overweight woman asks me to dress her body, I

will say, "You can't remain 450 pounds. Forget about picking the best clothes for your size; we can always help you look your prettiest, but it's just not healthy to weigh that much."

For the last three seasons, I've worked with finalists of *The Biggest Loser*, helping the contestants to dress their new bodies. They're still not small, but they're certainly half the size they were. And they are so much healthier. But they are faced with a fashion conundrum, because most of them haven't even been in a department store in years. They've just been home in their sweatpants. Now that they have so many decisions to make, they find the amount of choice almost debilitating.

These inspiring individuals are wonderful to work with, but I will say the men are often very difficult. They don't want to try anything new. They don't know what looks good on them, and they get into ruts. They don't want anything that remotely fits. "It's too confining!" they cry. "It's too constraining!"

I have to say to them, "Listen, sister. Get over it. That's what it feels like when a pair of pants fit."

I'm always shocked by how conservative people can be when it comes to their looks. The worst hairdo ever was the eighties puffy bangs. It wasn't good then, but everyone had it, so you could kind of forgive it. Now there are no excuses.

When I did *The Oprah Show* recently, I helped do makeovers on seven men. They were great with the clothes, totally game. But oh my, when the grooming people came in, it was another story. "You're not touching a hair on my head!" they yelled. "You're not touching a hair on my face!" As if they looked so incredibly fantastic being hairy like that.

I am always shocked by that kind of attitude. We're talking about *hair*, folks. It grows back! If you want to be Grizzly Adams again, you can. But I've noticed that when people take the risk, they often like what they find. In the case of one man on *Oprah,* there was a whole new person under all that hair, and he was actually pretty hot!

I said this on *Oprah:* If Mother Nature had her way, men and women would both turn into a giant bush. You have to pay attention to the messages you're sending out. I think unruly facial hair shows insecurity, or a real disregard for one's image.

Nose hair is a plague on our culture. Men need to keep in mind that there's hair growing from *everywhere.* Tweezing, wax- ing . . . there are tools—little electric things can be put into ears and noses. It's not painful. Everyone needs an additional mirror to help see these things. In our city, we spend a lot of time standing cheek by jowl with others, and it's hard not to notice when a bush is growing out of someone's ear.

These guys I met on *Oprah* were in their late thirties, early forties, and still wearing clothes from college. It was a Peter Pan complex, basically. They didn't want to grow up.

I see parents dressing like their children sometimes, and it disturbs me. When we do fashion shows at malls and the juniors' items come out, I deliver the opposite of a parental advisory warning. I say, "If you are over the age of sixteen, look away! These clothes are not for you."

From a fashion perspective, I find men are often averse to grooming because it puts their masculinity in jeopardy.

Men in Europe are more comfortable in their skin—or maybe it's just that they're more secure in their manhood. Men flirt with one another in France. They don't want to go to bed together, but they don't feel like their identity is threatened by finding another man attractive.

A strong division of gender roles is so pervasive in America, and I think it's dangerous. Liz Claiborne Inc. does a lot of consciousness-raising around domestic violence causes, and one day I contributed to the cause by doing a series of interviews on the topic with bloggers.

One of my questioners told me that she draws a line in the sand regarding gender. She said only men could be abusers. She said we have to take the boys aside and tell them how not to do it and the girls aside and say how not to let it happen to them.

"Everyone needs to know how to recognize whether they've become a victim or a perpetrator," I said. "*Everyone*, regardless of gender, needs to know both sides of this."

"I would never talk to a girl about how to avoid being an abuser," she said.

Well, I call that sheer ignorance. She's not looking at the bigger issues. I'm very pro co-ed everything. Everyone needs the same messages. Each gender's interested in what the other's doing. We need to tell everyone everything. What they choose to pay attention to is their issue, not ours.

In America, there's so much pressure to be straight that if men even have warm feelings for someone of the same sex, they suddenly feel they must watch *Girls Gone Wild* on repeat until they've proven they're not gay. I feel sorry for them, actually, because that's a lot of stress to be under. We're none of us all one thing all the time.

Maybe these guys just don't want to be vulnerable in that way, to put themselves on the line by doing some work on the way they look? Jerry Seinfeld famously said, "People think I'm gay because I'm single, I'm thin, and I'm neat."

Well, straight men, relax! I know just as many gay men who are big slobs. The rules of attraction dictate that you should cut your fingernails, toenails, and hair. Because I have sensitive skin, I try to skip shaving at least one day a week, but I try to pick a day when I'm only doing groceries and hanging around my house.

Self-interest and grooming intersect. Even if you don't like it, wouldn't you do it just to make sure you don't repel people who might go to bed with you? If heterosexual males are trying to attract a heterosexual female, shouldn't they maybe at least try to smell nice?

The question is what level of dressing up and grooming is appropriate for the occasion? What you need to do for a wedding versus what you do to go to the movies is different, but you should maintain a decent baseline standard.

Does grooming take time? Yes, it does. But we need to make a commitment. Taking a shower takes time, but if you never take one, you won't be invited out very much, so you'll have plenty of time left over. Should you ever blow off showers? Maybe if you're in a coma . . . but no, in that case someone will bathe you.

New parents are almost as bad about this as macho men. I hear from a lot of mothers of young children: "I don't have time."

I say, "If you think about your family as a brand, are you not a brand ambassador?" When I see frumpy mothers with impeccably turned-out children, I think they're making their children the family ambassadors, and that's too much pressure on someone who still picks her nose. And it's simply not occasion appropriate for a little child to be on the jungle gym in couture.

Speaking of inappropriate, have you seen all the tabloid photos of three-year-old Suri Cruise wearing heels? It's outrageous. People say, "She's setting a fashion standard." I say, "Preposterous!"

At *three*? It's not appropriate. If you're going to the playground to play, you should wear sneakers—Mary Janes at the very most.

Now, I liked playing dress-up just as much as the next kid, and men's clothes are boring to dress up in, so I think all children should have free range on their mothers' heels. But there's a difference between a child playing dress-up and a toddler seriously wearing high heels in her size while out in the world. I agree with the people who have said it sexualizes her. High heels are meant to make women look longer and leaner. That's not necessary for little girls. We don't want alluring little girls. There's something sick about it.

You don't need to—in fact, you shouldn't—wear cocktail dresses twenty-four hours a day. You can wear anything, as long as you wear it well. It just comes down to silhouette, proportion, and fit. At every age. You can be in jeans and a T-shirt, but you'll look good if you're paying attention to the shape and size that's right for you. Besides, baggy clothing is dangerous. Isadora Duncan was strangled by her long scarf when it got caught in the wheel spokes of a sports car. Let that be a lesson to us all.

As much as I encourage people to dress appropriately for events, I will grant that invites these days can be confusing. Dress instructions can be murky. People seem to stretch to think of new instructions. Fortunately for women, "black tie" no longer means a floor-length gown. It just means dressy. For a man it means a tuxedo. "Formal" to me means the same thing as "black tie," so why not just say "black tie"? "Semiformal," I assume, means a suit and a tie for a man and a nice dress for a woman.

The kind of thing I don't like is a mash-up like "festive formal." I guess it means a man could wear a bright-colored tie and cummerbund, and a woman could wear a dress that is both nice and fun?

Well, it's too much for me. I want to be comfortable, so if I see "festive formal," I'll just dress black tie and let other people be festive. If someone's going to break out some amazing dress, they'll do it whether or not they have the "festive" go-ahead, but for the rest of us, we're just confused.

When I was asked to present at the 2010 People's Choice Awards, the invitation specified "Hollywood chic." What in the world does that mean? I wore a suit.

But nothing's as bad as "black tie" during the daytime. I've seen it, and it's totally wrong on every level. Technically, if it's formal and daytime, men should not wear a tuxedo but rather a morning coat, but who owns tails? Nobody. Even I don't own tails, and if anyone in New York would have such a thing, I would. There should be no such thing as black tie in the daytime. It's not correct! If a man does it correctly with the morning coat, he'll look like he's in an Edwardian costume.

There is a way to clarify weird instructions on invitations. If I'm confused, I will call the host or the planner and ask, "What's expected?"

Weddings vary so much depending on where they're being held. If it's on a beach, you could do a sundress, but if it's in a church, you're probably going to want to cover your shoulders. There is an old rule about not wearing either black or white as a guest to a wedding, but I think black can be done if it's a party dress rather than something that looks like you're in mourning. In general, I think it's not a good idea to wear black to a wedding, but it's not a bitch-slap the way wearing white is.

There is a legendary story in the fashion world about the high-fashion Sykes sisters. Alexander McQueen was doing a wedding dress for Plum, but then her wedding was called off. She asked the designer to do a dress she could wear to her sister Lucy's wedding instead.

Well, a lot of people said it was her own wedding dress dyed black. She was furious and insisted she was not "the crazy, wedding-dress-wearing psycho-chick" the tabloids made her out to be. It was a unique dress, she said, and made for her as her sister's attendant.

Fair enough, although the dramatic floor-length dress did echo her twin sister's wedding dress, but in chocolate brown metallic chiffon, overlaid with lace. So maybe the moral is that if your twin sister is getting married, avoid chiffon, lace, and dark colors lest you be labeled a psycho by the tabloids.

What, you'd like some more universal thoughts on shopping?

The truth is, I buy my own suits off the rack from places like Banana Republic or Hugo Boss. I really can't afford a tailor. Those Tom Ford bespoke suits are $5,000–$6,000. People might want to spend that kind of money, but it's never necessary. You don't have to spend a ton of money to look good. And when it comes to shopping, even incredibly rich people have trouble finding what they want half the time, as I learned when I went shopping with two fabulously wealthy women.

Charities are always auctioning me off. The wife of a record mogul purchased me for lunch and a shopping trip. I usually take people to the Bryant Park Grill and then to Saks Fifth Avenue or Bloomingdale's, but this auction winner wanted to go to Bergdorf Goodman. So we had lunch there, which I'd never done before. It was expensive but very nice.

My auction winner brought a friend, and they were both extremely attractive women with great figures. One had as her goal a basic black top that would go with a black sequined cigarette pant. The winner was trying to find an upbeat holiday party dress. Three hours later . . . no luck.

The auction winner put on a $14,000 Yves St. Laurent dress.

"What do you think?" I asked.

"I don't hate it," she said.

"Off!" I insisted. "For fourteen thousand dollars, you are not allowed to say, 'I don't hate it.'"

We had people on all the floors looking for us. Luxury retailers in general have been so upset by the recession that they are acting in a very friendly way. I read in the *New York Times* about an everyday shopper who went to a luxury jewelry store on Madison Avenue and was offered a glass of champagne.

But the recession brings with it a major problem for shoppers: the dearth of inventory. Stores don't want to get stuck with extra merchandise, so they often don't have everyone's size. My incredulity was vocal. "It's the temple of high taste. These women want to spend lots of money. What's the problem?"

The thing we kept hearing was, "We're between the seasons. The holiday delivery is over. We're waiting for cruise."

It wasn't even Thanksgiving yet!

Finally, the auction winner said she would just go buy some new black Manolos because they go with everything. Well, they didn't have her size.

Whenever people say, "I can't get my fashion right because I'm on a budget," I say, "Guess what? Even if you have an unlimited budget, sometimes you can't do it."

I'd also like to encourage you to use this anecdote as your

own if you're ever around people who are flaunting their wealth and talking about buying expensive things. Just say: "I go shopping all the time. I'm *trying* to spend money. I mean, I tried on this fourteen-thousand-dollar Yves St. Laurent dress and thought: *I don't hate it.* Then I thought, *At least I can leave with a pair of Manolos,* but they didn't have my size!"

When it comes to strategic shopping, I love a surgical strike. I believe in knowing what it is you want. If it's a lot of things, go with a list. Don't get distracted by what's around you.

I don't like shopping if I'm looking for something specific. I'd rather do that kind of thing online. But I like doing shopping research, seeing what's out there at the stores. I look at all the fashion shows, but it doesn't necessarily translate to what the buyers are buying.

Speaking of which, do you know what the buyers are buying? Crocs.

I can't imagine a more aesthetically offensive item of footwear than Crocs. That little strap! I shudder.

Plus, they're dangerous. I was at Bloomingdale's and saw a little girl sobbing because the escalator had eaten her shoe. The charms (yes, there are charms that one can purchase to embellish those dreadful hunks of plastic) get caught on things, too. I've yet to see any condition where Crocs look good, including the beach. Why not flip-flops? I know Crocs are affordable. Well, so are Converse and lots of other brands that don't look like hooves.

But who knows? I came around somewhat to Uggs. I used to put Crocs and Uggs in the same sentence, but I don't anymore. The Ugg brand has evolved. They do some much more fashionable things now. I'm not as despondent.

I know I'm in the minority on this. The Crocs people are laughing all the way to the bank. Their profits were up something like 500 percent last year. You'll still never catch me dead wearing them, even if it is a "casual Friday."

Casual Fridays are an invitation for people to go too far. One day I went to visit the Parsons board chairman, whom I'd seen only in a suit. There he was in dad jeans—flood pants to boot—and a polo shirt that was way too big. I hadn't realized it was casual Friday. It was like being the only person not told about Opposite Day. In any case, I was appalled.

The other thing that makes me crazy is the bare midriff. It's a don't-let-this-happen-to-you-ever category of problem. I loved the Season 7 *Curb Your Enthusiasm* episode entitled "The Bare Midriff," in which a woman named Maureen goes around the office in a tiny shirt that reveals her whole stomach—and what they call a muffin top. Larry says she's not dressing appropriately and would she please wear a longer shirt. Maureen gets very defensive and says, "I've lost sixty-eight pounds in two years. I'm very proud and I want to flaunt what I've got!"

At a gym, a bare midriff is fine. I've never been in a gym—well, not since high school. I'm sure there are all kinds of things there that are just fine because they stay *there*. Things can happen around a pool or at a beach that wouldn't happen in a formal dining room.

At the office, though, no matter what kind of shape you're in, showing off that much of your body isn't right. These days, though, I see accidental bare midriffs more often than intentional ones.

Low-rise jeans are great, but ladies, you need a belt, or a tunic, or a unitard. I say this to women all the time who are very pear-shaped: wear a low-rise jean, because if it fits you in the hip it won't fit you in the waist. Just wear a top that covers the waistband.

Otherwise, anytime you bend over, everyone sees everything. One of our segment producers is adorable, but she's so whatever's-whatever about belts and things that I've seen almost every part of her anatomy.

I find myself yelling, "Please don't bend over. I'll get it!"

And you know what's funny: I've never heard a woman acknowledge that she'd just flashed me. I think it's so common now.

Doing as many makeovers as I do, I've learned a few things about what makes women feel better about themselves. The starting point is usually getting a new haircut. I don't want to generalize, because every case is different, but I think it's best to err on the side of styling your hair shorter the older you get. In my opinion, it's generally not a good look for women over thirty to have hair way below their shoulders.

I LOVE WRITING MY fashion advice column for *Marie Claire*. Those are real questions. One question I received was from a woman who said she had a Hervé Leger dress in dark purple, which I assume was the famous Leger color aubergine. She was wearing it to a swanky Beverly Hills engagement party with a beige patent-leather peep-toe stiletto. Her mother said her clutch should match the shoes, and my questioner asked if that was indeed the case.

I began by saying I love Hervé Leger and I love aubergine, but why would you wear beige with that? Matching is hard. Make it easy on yourself. Go with a metallic! Beige dresses things down. Really, a good rule is no beige after five.

If it's after five, people call it "nude," but that's not in my vocabulary because it's a racist color name. Depending on what your skin tone is, that beigy color may or may not be nude.

Now, wearing a true nude, meaning matching your skin color, is a whole different matter. You usually look odd, I think. It's like a body suit even when it's a voluminous dress. Kirsten Dunst does that all the time, and I don't consider her a fashion role model. (Sorry, Kirsten.)

You don't know what colors work for you until you try a bunch of things on. If you're pale and you look at Iman and think, *That color's fantastic on her. I'm going to get that dress,* stop right there!

Dark women are blessed in many ways, because they have so many more colors that look great on them. Lighter women don't know it, but there aren't as many colors that work with fair skin.

So try to think outside the box and try on colors you would never consider. You'll probably be surprised that some unexpected color—persimmon, coral, or teal—works like magic with your skin.

And don't worry about the so-called rules of colors. The No White after Labor Day rule was meant to be broken. But it's true that white is not very practical in New York City. I have a pair of white jeans that the J. Crew catalog convinced me to buy. What I learned once I put them on: thin white pants need to be lined, because otherwise they reveal the line between your leg and your underpants, and that's not my favorite look. The jeans have languished in my closet.

What's another "rule": Don't wear black and brown together? That's ridiculous. You do have to be careful about the brown. It shouldn't be tan or some midtone, but chocolate brown is really chic. I once saw a woman on the street wearing chocolate suede boots with black opaque tights and a black dress. She looked fantastic.

I will say that I think it's funny that strangers take my fashion advice when my own family completely ignores it. Case in point: During the holiday season, my family wears Christmas sweaters every single day. Christmas sweaters! Is there a bigger fashion don't?

But for those of you who do listen to me, here's my general advice about keeping your wardrobe fresh: It's helpful just to drop into stores and try things on for information whenever you think of it. It's essential to get a sense of what cuts and colors look best on you, and you can't always do that when you have to find a dress for a wedding during your lunch hour. You can learn so much just by asking yourself objectively, "Does this look good on me?"

Size is difficult, because different brands run small or large. So you're likely to have a range, 8–10 say, or 2–4, or 14–16. But if you don't spend the time figuring out your range, you're likely to be very frustrated each time you go shopping, because you won't even know what sizes to pick off the rack.

Figuring these things out is just a part of everyday life.

You know how I am about all these matters. You can reject any or all of what I say, obviously. These are just the things that I think are good rules of thumb for enjoying your life as a social being. I also have no problem if you want to find a cave and have someone roll a boulder in front of it. To each his own.

In a recent memoir about filming *Some Like It Hot,* the 1959 comedy with Marilyn Monroe, Tony Curtis says at first he was resistant to dressing in drag for the role. He was a sex symbol and was embarrassed that he had to put on a dress.

But then when he did, he had a new concern: He wasn't pretty enough! He and his costar, Jack Lemmon, went back to the wardrobe people and demanded better makeup, higher heels, and bigger falsies. His logic: If he was going to be a girl, he was going to be a pretty girl, by God.

That's how people should be about everything: whatever you're doing, give it your all.

That's one of the things I love about *Project Runway*. It's about each designer being the best at whatever it is he or she wants to do.

Whenever I do makeovers, I like to bring out whatever it is in that person of which they are most proud. I hate almost all makeover shows, because they tend to make everyone look the same: still frumpy, but slightly more upscale and slightly more put together than before.

I like to learn about the person and to find out how she really wants to look, what energy she wants to put out into the world. You can see it in the eyes of the people at the end of the show: they feel like they had a hand in the process, and the look they end up with is really *them*. It's not just a costume. It's about who you are and how you want to be perceived.

When I did a photo shoot for *More* magazine, we had two female lawyers, very different body types. I asked one of them, Karen, "Do you think you're Hillary Clinton?" All she had were these very masculine pantsuits. She looked so dowdy and off-putting. When I told her this, she said, "I'm fifty-four years old. Aren't I *supposed* to be dowdy?"

"No! No! No!" I told her. I don't believe anyone ever has to look dowdy, and it's perplexing when they do.

But when it came down to what direction to take her in, I was confused. I took her sister aside and said, "Talk to me. Karen is working a very strong masculine look. In fact, is this who she is?" I didn't want to put her in flowery prints if she was more of a truck-driver gal.

"I don't think so," she said, "but I'm confused by it, too."

This was interesting, because I'd half expected the sister to say, "Yes, she's a diesel dyke." And then we'd have worked with that. But that wasn't the case here.

So I took Karen aside and said, "What's going on here? Are these really the clothes you like wearing? Is this pantsuit *you*?"

"No" she told me, "but I don't know how to be professional as a woman and not dress this way." She was in court all the time and felt she had to convey authority. "I'd love to look more feminine, but I just don't know how."

In my first book, *Tim Gunn: A Guide to Quality, Taste & Style*, I talked about style mentors. It's great to look around and find people in movies or books or pop culture whose style you want to emulate. Is it Audrey Hepburn, Debbie Harry, or *Law & Order*'s Mariska Hargitay? It's helpful to think of your icon when you are constructing your own personal style. But this lawyer was just looking to male lawyers to construct her look.

I told her, "You're wearing menswear-tailored clothing. Matching jackets and pants. There are other ways to look professional, you know. Right now you don't look professional. I wouldn't be drawn to you—unless I saw you at a leather bar."

Luckily, she was open to showing off her figure and trying new things. She instantly had a whole new world available to her. Well, the transformation was thrilling. She felt unshackled. She realized that it's looking good that makes you comfortable and confident, not just wearing casual or shape-less clothing.

Now she has the courtroom in her pocket, because she looks so much more accessible and she's so much surer of herself. And still she gets to wear her favorite leather pants on the weekend.

RULE 9

Talk to Me: There's Always Another Side to the Story

WHEN I WAS BACKSTAGE waiting to present at the 2010 People's Choice Awards, I encountered the stunning Kate Walsh from *Private Practice* and *Grey's Anatomy*. She was wearing an incredibly cute vintage Count Ferdinando Sarmi beaded dress, but the effect of the dress was compromised by her demeanor as she talked on the phone.

"That person is a *seat filler!*" she was yelling at the person on the other end.

Apparently, her boyfriend arrived at their seats and saw that there were people already sitting in them. Rather than identifying himself to an usher as having been assigned that seat, he got on the phone and yelled at Kate, who was waiting backstage until it was her turn to present.

"They're not allowed to have an empty seat!" she was yelling at him. "Those are our seats!"

It seemed fairly simple, but she didn't seem to be getting through to him. She got off the phone and said, "I have to leave and go talk to my boyfriend."

"You can't leave," the backstage staff said. "You're about to present."

I turned to my agent, Jonathan Swaden, and said, "She's too fabulous for this. She needs to start going out with some people who can take care of themselves."

It was high drama.

But I really did think there was a lesson in there about taking care of yourself and making others take care of themselves. Suddenly, she was expected to help her boyfriend navigate the seating rules rather than do her job and introduce an award on national television.

The boyfriend needed to recognize that there was another side to the story he thought he had figured out. The old expression is totally true: "If you assume, you make an ass out of you and me."

That applies in a professional context as well.

We have an amazing library at Liz Claiborne Inc. called the Design and Merchandising Resource Center, which falls under my authority as chief creative officer. Well, sometimes designers borrow textiles and then never return them, or return them in terrible condition. Expensive books vanish. And then when I ban them from borrowing things, they plead persecution!

Call me a schoolmarm, but few things make me angrier than people not taking good care of library materials. This was edited out on *Project Runway*, but at the Metropolitan Museum of Art challenge in Season 7, I lost my patience with the designers when they kept trying to put their paws all over some of the Costume Institute's most delicate treasures.

Speaking of museums, there was one perfect moment in Project Runway's Season 6: we went to the amazing J. Paul Getty Museum in Los Angeles, but it almost didn't happen.

The Getty invited us, and I was just thrilled. I love that museum. But the powers that be were not as eager to go there. The Weinstein Company and Lifetime were saying, "But in Season Four you went to the Metropolitan Museum of Art!"

In a conference call with the producers, who supported going to the Getty, and with TWC and Lifetime, who did not, I said I couldn't believe they were going to keep us from going to a museum just because we'd been to one before. "Are you telling me if we were in Paris we couldn't go to the Louvre?" I said.

Luckily, the producers and I won, and we went. It was amazing. The mayor of Los Angeles greeted us. We saw the sun rise there. The designers had the run of the whole place. It was phenomenal. And I seriously doubt that while we were navigating the glorious galleries and outdoor spaces of the Getty, anyone at home complained about our having been to a museum in the past.

I find with complaints in general, you need to know the whole context, including what the expectation was. So frequently, I've found that the expectation has been totally false, a creation of the person's own imagination. They're disappointed not to get something they were never promised.

I had this happen with my students. They would call their parents to complain about school, and then I would hear about it from the angry parents. But the parents didn't know the administration's side. They would be furious that we weren't accepting their child's project, but they did not know that the child had missed multiple deadlines. Why don't parents do their own probing? "Tell me more," they should say to Junior. "Why wouldn't they accept it? Do you really not know why?"

I always wondered at the students who allowed their parents to get so involved. When I was in my twenties, I did as much as I could on my own. My parents were generous when they felt they needed to be, but I had enough of an ego that I would turn down their help whenever possible.

The key is admitting that in every situation there's a lot you don't know. That's hard for me sometimes, because I like being an authority. But realizing I can see only a tiny piece of the puzzle is surprisingly liberating.

My father helped me stay humble on this front by being very mysterious my whole life. He was almost never around. He worked constantly. My mother and grandmother were there day in and day out. So when I got into trouble, I always expected my mother would be there and my father would be absent, as usual. But the opposite was true. My father was always great in a crisis.

And I sure did provide my family with plenty of crises. I constantly had issues. He was always there. He was there as a support, not to slap me around and ask me what the matter with me was. He just showed up and took care of business and did whatever he could to help. When I really needed a father, he was there. People who are by your side all the time, like my mother and grandmother—you'd think they'd rally, but they sometimes fall apart. My father could be hundreds of miles away on business, but then suddenly he was there. I'll always be grateful to him for that. And I'll always think of him as an example of how people can surprise you for the better.

Of course, they can also surprise you for the worse.

I'm reminded of a celebrated young designer. People think he's a tremendous talent, and he is, but there's another side to the story.

Few people know this, but this designer was dismissed for

academic dishonesty. The trouble started when some of his classmates told me he wasn't turning in his own work. Again, there are two sides to every story, so I went to talk to his teachers.

"I understand there's a problem," I said.

"That's news to me," the teachers responded.

I almost let it drop there, but owing to this uprising from the students, I thought, *I at least have to have a discussion with the student.*

I had my associate Marsha join me, and we sat down with him in my office.

"I've heard accusations against you from your peers," I began. "How do you respond to the claim that you've copied work?"

He was staring off into space and looking around.

"It's either true or it's not true, or it's true with mitigating circumstances," I said. "Talk to me. Tell me what's going on."

"It's true," he admitted. "It's not my work."

He went on to tell me that he hadn't turned in any of his own work since the beginning of his junior year. He was collecting projects from wherever he could find them—including those from former students, or muslins left lying on tables. He explained that he didn't have time to do school projects because he was so eager to get out into the real world.

"Well, I'm going to give you plenty of time," I told him. "Effective immediately, you are dismissed from this school for academic dishonesty."

This fellow has since had great success, and I'm happy for him. He is incredibly talented. And yet, I've always felt a twinge of annoyance when I encounter his work.

One celebrity dress of his attracted an especially great deal of attention. The day after photos of the dress appeared in the papers, a colleague of mine called me to say she wished the celebrity had worn a dress by a different designer.

Recalling the copycat history, I lowered my voice and replied, "How do you know she didn't?"

Be a Good Guest or Stay Home (I Won't Judge You—I Hate Parties)

THESE DAYS, I DON'T have much free time, and when I do, I want to close the door and sit in the dark. If I have a friend over, I usually just brew a pot of coffee, and if I'm feeling very festive, then we'll have sherry and I'll throw some Toll House cookies on a baking sheet.

Don't make fun, foodies! Breaking those things apart requires strength. The last time I made them I had a horrible time separating the dough, so even though I didn't whip anything up from *Gourmet,* I had a feeling of real accomplishment when they came out of the oven. My guest and I both enjoyed them tremendously.

But I definitely have made the party rounds, and I'll tell you about a few illustrative occasions.

One evening I went to a very memorable dinner party. It was held at a grand New York City apartment. The place was beautiful, elegantly furnished, and full of contemporary art. I was quite impressed.

When I arrived, they were serving cocktails, and I was having a nice time. But the cocktail hour just went on and on . . .

and on. There was nothing to snack on, so people were starting to get rather tipsy. I didn't drink very much, but I was starting to think: *Is there a nut or pretzel around here? If I don't eat something, I'm going to have trouble seeing straight.*

I assumed they weren't seating people for dinner because not everyone was there yet. If I hear I'm supposed to arrive at seven thirty for dinner, I think dinner will probably be served around eight, so the window to arrive is between seven thirty and eight, and preferably on the early side of that. If you arrive at 7:59, you are really pushing it. I arrived at this dinner at around seven thirty-five or seven forty. But people were dribbling in until nine p.m. The martinis were really flowing, and everyone was getting completely smashed.

Now, I grew up in a family of excessive drinkers. There wasn't a single holiday gathering when some item of furniture didn't break. One year it was an uncle putting his foot through a coffee table. I was a kid, so I didn't totally comprehend what was happening. But I remember the dinner being cleared and everyone smoking and someone saying, "Does anyone want an after-dinner drink?" and everyone saying, "Yes, a martini!"

Now that I'm an adult, I know that a martini is not an after-dinner drink. It's a getting-the-party-started drink. As it turned out, even though my family members had been drinking since five p.m., after dinner they really got started!

Anyway, back to this memorable dinner party: after a good two hours of drinking in a way that would do my family proud, we finally sat down to dinner and were each presented with a steamed artichoke with butter dipping sauce. Also, of course, plenty of wine.

Then the artichoke went away, and I thought, *Lovely first course.* Then this teeny container of sorbet came out a few minutes later. I thought it was a palate cleanser, but no, the sorbet was dessert. Meal over.

I thought: *Are these hosts so bombed that they forgot there's a chicken in the oven?* But I didn't smell anything cooking. Some of the guests were making eye contact with one another as if to ask: *Is this really it?* But nothing was said, and the party ended not long after dinner. I think we all hit McDonald's on the way home.

The next day, I sent a note. I don't lie, but I can be diplomatic and disguise things in politeness. I told the truth and said it was "an unforgettable party."

I received an e-mail back that said, "We so enjoyed having you there and thanks so much for coming!"

What I really expected to hear back was, "Thank you. We were so embarrassed when we later realized we forgot to serve the roast." There was never any acknowledgment about the mysteriously sparse meal. I'm constantly thinking there must be an answer to the sphinx. You wouldn't sit down at a table formally set with silverware with no food to serve, would you?

I actually was thinking about that modest dinner at a lunch I attended at the White House on July 24, 2009. I was even seated at Mrs. Obama's table, which was a tremendous thrill for me. She is such a fashion icon and has amazing presence. (At the lunch, she was wearing Michael Kors. I just love how she supports American designers.)

The first course that came out was a tiny salad. The main course was crab cakes the size of silver dollars with cannellini beans and grilled summer squash from the White House garden. A lovely woman sitting next to me made some comment to a table companion about how teeny the portions were, and Mrs. Obama overheard and chose to address it.

"When we arrived at the White House," she said, "I could not believe how wasteful we were in what we served people and how much we threw away. I'd rather have people leave lunch and go get an ice-cream cone than to throw away so much food."

Indeed, everyone ate everything. Not an ounce of food went to waste. And I really liked her attitude. First of all, how classy was it that she frankly and warmly addressed an overheard complaint? Mrs. Obama made the guests feel comfortable and taken care of. No one starved. We're so used to these huge portions, but they're not necessary. It wasn't a ton of food, and indeed I did grab a little snack that afternoon, but the food was very tasty, the company was excellent, and unlike my artichoke friends' meal, the lunch consisted of three courses!

PERHAPS YOU REMEMBER HOW at the Obamas' first State Dinner there were two crashers, a couple who wanted to be a part of the *Real Housewives of Washington, D.C.* I won't mention their names because they've gotten enough newsprint already. As you'll probably recall, they managed to wheedle their way into this exclusive party in spite of not being on the guest list (though they claim a misunderstanding). They even got close to President Obama and Vice President Biden.

Well, I was truly shocked by this on all levels.

Speaking as one who merely went to lunch at the White House, I simply can't fathom how anyone could get in without being invited. When I went, the layers of security were intense.

Several weeks before the lunch, I had to fill out a questionnaire, giving my Social Security number and my date and place of birth. I even had to call my mother and find out the name of the hospital where I was born. (It was the since closed Columbia Hospital for Women in Washington, D.C., for those of you who like those sorts of details.)

At the check-in when I reached the White House, one of my fellow guests arrived with a surprise date. (The audacity!)

The staff was lovely to the uninvited guest and said, "We are so sorry we are not able to have you attend, but we have a sitting room where you may wait for your friend, and we'd be happy to bring you a plate."

There were many more checkpoints between the door and the event. The final obstacle was the first lady's chief of staff, Susan Sher, who waited at the top of the stairs with the guest list.

It was probably the tenth time I saw the list. Luckily, I was still on it, and she recognized me and greeted me warmly. It was only then that I relaxed. It was such an elaborate process, I was nervous that they weren't going to let me in!

And yet somehow these horrid party crashers were able to waltz right into the first State Dinner of the administration. What kind of message are these reality-show hoodlums sending to our young people? "You feel like going to the White House? Dress up and head on over there!"

Where is the penalty for that kind of brazenness? What kind of culture do we live in where someone can say, "I want it, so I'm going to have it now—circumstances be damned"?

People like this want the cheaper version of fame: celebrity. They want to be famous, but not for having done anything. That's the opposite of what I think our young people need to be taught, which is: It's wonderful to aspire to things. Aspire to be invited to the White House. Maybe one day you will be.

To accomplish such a feat, it's very important to practice good qualities of character.

Shortly after the crasher scandal, I was interviewed by a blogger who sees these crashers as national heroes.

"It's what we all should be doing," she said.

"Ha-ha-ha-ha," I responded.

"I'm not joking," she replied. "I'm altogether serious."

"This is egregious behavior," I asserted. "It's the White House and the president. It's a State Dinner. One doesn't crash the White House. One doesn't crash a wedding. One doesn't crash anything that's invitation only."

"It shouldn't be exclusive," she said.

"What?" I said with incredulity. "They're private events!" I wondered if she thought Andrew Jackson's 1829 inauguration, at which the public showed up at the White House ball and trashed the place, was a good model. "Are you just trying to get a rise out of me?" I asked.

She assured me that she was not.

"What do you say to your children?" I inquired, fearing the answer.

"I tell them: 'You go wherever you want to go! You do whatever you want to do!'"

I said I thought that underscored a dangerous sense of entitlement. Young people need guidelines. What are they going to do? Just arrive at orientation at Harvard and say they want to go there and so they will, even though they haven't been accepted and haven't paid tuition?

"What's your feeling about domestic violence?" I asked. "Is anyone entitled to act out in any way?" (I was being interviewed about Liz Claiborne Inc.'s support of domestic violence prevention programs before we'd veered off to talk about the crashers.)

"Having been on the receiving end of domestic violence, I don't feel that way," she said.

"Well," I said, "you have experience that tells you otherwise. Maybe if you were the host of an invitation-only dinner party and people whom you weren't expecting showed up and you had no place to seat them, you would realize that's wrong."

I still believe that to be true, even if people like those terrible White House party crashers are constantly providing a counterexample in which trashy behavior is rewarded. To cheer myself up, I try to remember the difference between short-term and long-term success. Living a really good life and making a real mark on society is a marathon, not a sprint.

NOW, BACK TO REGULAR old parties. I confess to you, and I'm somewhat ashamed of this: I don't particularly like entertaining. I know I should, but I just don't.

I love cooking. I cook for myself every day. I like the ceremony of it. It takes me into a different zone. I make a lot of pasta and meat loaf (ground chicken or turkey and only occasionally ground beef). Rather than buying in bulk, I just grocery shop every day. I know my rate of consumption, and that way I can just pick up some produce and whip something up. I haven't bought red meat in a long time. I'd like to say it's because I'm so ecologically conscious, but the truth is, I can't make a good steak.

But cooking for a crowd of five or ten or, heaven forbid, twenty?

No, thank you. I don't like feeling like a slave to the care and feeding of my guests. Whenever I've had parties, I'm in the kitchen mixing drinks for the entire evening, and I never actually get to enjoy and converse with anyone. Maybe that's why the only people I see with any regularity are my friends the Banus, who drink only champagne. It makes hosting so easy. All I have to do is say, "Want some more?" and pour away.

Honestly—and maybe some of you can relate to this—I just can't stand the pressure of being responsible for hosting a memorable (and not in a bad way) evening. Martha Stewart, bless her heart, intimidates me. That level of entertaining is so over my head: *What do you mean, you didn't dig up your own potatoes for this dish? You didn't make the doilies? The plates didn't just come out of a kiln?*

I love Martha, but it gets ridiculous.

And yet, I have learned a few things in my many years of party attendance.

Bad weather is good for parties. You get only those people who really want to be there.

Entertaining shouldn't be about showing off. It's all about making people feel comfortable and setting a stage for everyone to have a good time, make new friends, and have stimulating conversations. You want to leave a party thinking: *If I hadn't gone to that, I never would have met this wonderful person, or had that delicious meal, or felt that sense of camaraderie with the people I met at the dessert table.* You don't want anyone looking at the clock, thinking, *When can I leave?*

NOW, WHERE ARE MY single ladies and men? It's hard, isn't it, when you don't have someone to take to a party full of couples? At office parties and certain events, there is pressure to bring someone. People are constantly trying to hook me up with dates, but I'd just as soon go alone.

Even my own mother (to whom I've never officially come out) says, "What about your old age? Don't you want to be with someone?"

Lately, I've started to say, sincerely, "Maybe not."

The truth is, I don't have time to be a good partner. Relationships take commitment, and all my energy goes into my work. I wouldn't want to let someone I cared about into my life and then never be home, or always be distracted. To be a good partner, I would have to give something up. What would it be?

There are a lot of perfectly happy single people in this city. It just matters who you are and what you want. And I would never want to be one of those serial monogamists who have a different partner every year and are always wondering why it never works out. Generally speaking, there's a reason why people can't sustain a long-term relationship. They think, *It can't be my fault,* when the odds are pretty good that they're doing something at least subconsciously that tells the world they're not ready to settle down. At least I *know* I don't want to settle down!

That's why parties where people are expected to bring a date even if they are single can be so stressful.

It's not quite as bad, though, as parties where people bring dates who *aren't* expected. That's one of the most egregious social sins anyone can commit. It's hugely presumptuous.

I've been at fairly small dinner parties to which someone's unexpectedly brought someone with an excuse like, "My sister was in town."

The host is typically accommodating but secretly seething.

Someone I know had people who showed up to her wedding who had not RSVP'd. She didn't have food for them or a place for them to sit, so she said, simply, "You should have told us you were coming," and sent them away. Good for her!

Fortunately, bad behavior by others can sometimes work to your advantage. At events with tables for ten someone sometimes shows up with an unexpected guest, and suddenly there are too few place settings. Usually, this is about the time I'm dreaming of being back home in front of the TV, so I will graciously say, "Please, take my seat! I will just disappear."

"No, please don't!" my tablemates will insist. "Stay!"

"No," I say gallantly, "things happen for a reason. I am happy to sacrifice for the good of the table." Meanwhile, I'm thinking, *I wonder if I can get home before* House Hunters International *starts?* (I watch a lot of HGTV.)

The only trick is: Don't look back. Keep going. Pray there's no coat check. Don't stop for a taxi. Get around the corner and then hail one.

Honestly, it's fun to get dressed up, but I prefer simpler affairs. I like it when I go to parties and there's a pitcher of something sitting out for people who don't know exactly what they want right away. And I like when you can just go get your second drink yourself. It frees up the host and lends an air of informality to things. Similarly, it's good to make dishes in advance so you can just heat them up.

I also like having at least one person around who is widely disliked among your crowd of lovely people. You never know who's going to get along with whom, but you do know people need *someone* to gossip about later, and you don't want it to be you.

My niece and I were just talking about Thanksgiving, and

she was saying there was someone she wasn't particularly looking forward to seeing.

"But if she weren't coming," I told my niece, "maybe you'd
be picking on me!" It's always good to have someone in that
pariah category, because they let the rest of us off the hook.

Maybe I'll start entertaining more since I just moved into a
more party-friendly apartment. For the first time in my adult-
hood, I have a dining room table. It's beautiful, and I love having it. But no one's ever sat at it. Maybe this will be the year I
actually start enjoying party giving . . . Or maybe I'll continue
to put my gorgeous dining room table to a slightly less social
use: doing crossword puzzles in my pajamas.

ALAS, UNLESS YOU ARE made of stronger stuff than I am,
there is no avoiding the holiday-party circuit. From what I can
tell, the holiday season is just an excuse for bad behavior. Party
season is like a military gauntlet, with cocktails being flung at
you instead of clubs.

I knew I had entered into a real state of Grinchdom when I
was chatting with the maintenance man who was putting up a
tree in the lobby of a company I was doing some work for and
heard myself say: "This tree looks like a metaphor for this company: anemic, ratty, and artificial."

Well, we bonded over our ambivalence about both our em-
ployer and the sorry state of the old plastic tree, and that was a
nice moment of holiday cheer—our laughter around the tree.
But, in general, I have trouble getting into the spirit.

I travel by train on the holidays. Leaving New York for Dela-
ware one year, there was a power outage on the tracks. It was
like the evacuation of postrevolutionary Russia. When power

was finally restored and the first train left the station, there was a cheer at Penn Station. Then they put four Acela trains together, and everyone was sitting on suitcases. We were just lucky to get out of there. My niece and I had been talking about how we were going to have a Merry Skype-mas, whereby we would all sit around our computers and talk with one another over the Internet rather than gathering under the same roof.

Well, once we arrived at our destination, it was one thing right after the other. My mother had a high blood pressure attack. She had to go to the emergency room and stay in the hospital for three days. That night, my nephew, Mac, took his parents' car to a party. At four a.m., the police were pounding on the door. The car was found in a ditch. Mac was in his room, covered with blood and mud.

My sister called me at a quarter to six in the morning from the emergency room to report on Mac's condition. I drove to the ER in Mother's car and picked them up. They didn't volunteer details, and I didn't ask, because I didn't want to have to tell my mother. I could honestly say that I knew nothing. Better that she should hear all about it from my sister.

Unfortunately, at a quarter to ten, my drama-queen niece called and told me the whole story before I could tell her I didn't want to know. So then when my mother asked what had happened, I had to fill her in. I could have faked ignorance, but as you know, I am pretty much incapable of telling a lie. Alas!

Wallace told me on the way back that she'd started out feeling sorry for Mac, then she felt sad for the family, and then she just felt mad. I said, "You should feel mad. Anger is good."

At the same time, it wasn't such a bad holiday season over all. Nobody died!

EVEN BEFORE THE HOSPITAL visits and car crashes, family get-togethers have been fraught. One year, my sister-in-law (she's my sister's husband's sister, if you like the details of convoluted relationships) used Thanksgiving dinner as an opportunity to fight with her brother about who would host their mother for Christmas.

"You led me to believe that she spent three days with you, but I happen to know she was only with you for a few hours," my sister-in-law said accusatorily.

"What?" my brother-in-law said. "We had her for three days."

"That's not the information I have," his sister said.

It's not as if this can't be verified one way or the other, and is Thanksgiving dinner really the time to do it?

When she behaves that way, she acts like she and the person she's speaking to are the only people in the room. I hate it when couples do that.

Quite a few years ago, when my niece and nephew were very young, old family friends joined us for our family Thanksgiving dinner. Owing to Wallace and Mac's young age, there were knock-knock jokes and probably some references to farting and other bodily noises.

One of the invited guests turned to her husband and stage-whispered, "Bob, would you please do something to ratchet up this conversation! I'm about to fall asleep from boredom."

I started to stew.

My sister was talking to my niece and nephew about whatever preteens are interested in, and meanwhile this lady is huffing and puffing dramatically.

Well, someone asked my sister something, and I said, "Wait! Before you answer, make sure you properly *ratchet up* the quality of your answer, because heaven forbid that our guest should be bored to such a degree that she falls into her plate of food!" With that, I threw down my napkin and stormed away from the table and upstairs to Mother's guest room.

The stage whisper is highly problematic. It's trying to do what you want to do without taking accountability. My grandmother was a master of it, and now my mother has taken up the torch. You criticize someone in the room without saying something to their face. It's rude. Think they can't hear you? They can. They're being polite enough to *pretend* that they can't.

There are four topics that should be completely avoided at all social events, and they are: religion, politics, finances, and sex. These things are, quite frankly, nobody's business. There is, however, an exception in New York: money is totally fair game.

I think that's because it's a very expensive city, and unless you find some luck, it's very hard to get by. On my teacher's salary, I did get a little panicky at times. Thank goodness that for the sixteen years I spent in the West Village, my landlords never once raised my rent. I paid $1,200 a month for that entire time. (Trust me: That was an absurd bargain for what I got, especially considering my neighbor was Sarah Jessica Parker, whom I adore.) I loved that apartment for the first thirteen of the sixteen years, until the disrepair spread to the point where it seemed dangerous. I thought the windows were going to fall out.

Anyway, before I even dreamed I would ever have the means to buy an apartment, Nina Garcia was complaining about the renovation of her new place. She was talking about how much it cost to redo the bathroom. I thought she said $17,000 and was aghast.

"No," she said, *"Seventy thousand dollars."*

I nearly fainted.

When I first moved to the city, I spent the first five years dumbstruck by questions about how much I'd paid for things. It's something you would never ask in Washington. You'd be considered a heathen, raised by wolves in a trailer park. And now I ask it! *How much is this apartment?*

Recently I was going down the hallway to my elevator. Standing there were two women. One was a Realtor, and the other was a client. I talked about my apartment and what it was like when I'd moved in and what I'd done to it. I was *this close* to asking, "How much is the apartment you're considering?" But I restrained myself. (Also, I remembered I could just go look it up on the real estate agent's Web site.)

Compulsively dropping the names of fabulous people you know is another New York social sport. As part of another charity auction, I was lunching with Liz Smith and the winning bidder. Liz brought with her a friend, the former head of an ad agency. The two of them did nothing but name-drop. That stuff rolls off me, but I felt bad for the winning woman and her daughter, who could never compete. They may have enjoyed the show, but I was worried they felt left out.

Now that I at last have a roomy apartment of my very own, I should really think about having guests more often. This is the first time I've ever had a bed bigger than a single. I've actually moved on up to a double bed, and I feel very decadent about it. And yet, I confess to you that I am such a hermit, it's hard for me to open my house up to other people. I consider my home a retreat and enjoy my monastic life. I'm a bit OCD about my environment. In New York you're up against people all day long, and when you get home you really need to re-charge.

When I do have guests, it usually goes fine, but I have to remember to do a thorough home orientation when the house-guest arrives. I imagine that Martha Stewart would say that if your house were set up properly, your guest wouldn't need an orientation. You need to look at your house through a stranger's eyes.

My niece, Wallace, was staying with me recently and depro-grammed my TV by trying to watch cable. Mysteriously, you have to be on "Component 1" rather than "TV." If only she'd asked. Anyway, I was sorry that she hadn't gotten a chance to watch her shows and also that the TV had to be reset.

But Wallace is a really good houseguest. I've also had some bad ones. A colleague of mine would send her husband and two kids up to their country place during the summer, and since she didn't want to go home to the suburbs during the summer by herself, for two summers she camped with me every week—Monday through Thursday—for three months.

I was living paycheck to paycheck and buying groceries for two. I would get home earlier than she would and would cook and leave her food. She would get home, collapse into a chair, and say, "Meat loaf again?" She never even bought a bottle of wine.

She was assuming a great deal about my love life. Wouldn't it be possible that I would want to have a guest over? She was right that I didn't have anyone in that category, but I could have.

I sat her down and explained that I couldn't sustain these

shenanigans another year. I implied that it was putting some restrictions on my own freedom. She came up with a compromise, whereby she would stay at my place for two nights and someone else's for two nights. I was too nice back then, and I said okay. But I'm strong enough now that I wouldn't welcome an open-ended stay anymore. My privacy is too important to me.

I've learned to keep my big mouth shut when someone says, "I'm coming to town for the weekend and looking for a place to stay!" or "I'd love to visit New York, but I can't afford a hotel!" Now I stay quiet or say something along the lines of, "Oh, too bad! Guess you'll have to stay home and save up!"

My mother's retirement place has separate guest rooms with baths. When I'm visiting, she always says, "Would you like to stay in one of the guest rooms rather than in my apartment?" I happen to know she's looking for affirmation that I would rather room with her. So I say, "Of course I'd rather stay with you, Mother," when in fact the thought of getting up and having coffee alone in the morning before the day of family time starts is pretty enticing.

I know a lot of people go through this same thing with their families, where every question is loaded. The appropriate answer to every question is: "What do you mean by that?" Everything has a subtext.

To be a good houseguest, you should be as independent as possible. You should buy groceries or take your hosts out for dinner. Pick up after yourself. Pretend to have a good time even if you're not. Say, "I'd like to make a dinner reservation tonight. What's your favorite restaurant?" Try not to break anything. Be quiet.

I read something interesting in *Martha Stewart Living*: If

you have a guest room, sleep in it to see what worldly needs your guest may have that aren't accommodated. But there are limits to how far I go. I don't have a television in my own bedroom, so I won't put one in the guest room. Besides, everyone can watch TV on the computer now. There's no need for guests from Denmark to use your landline to make a $60 phone call. They can Skype.

The only place I was ever a regular guest was in Hong Kong, with Suzy Moser and Chris Berrisford. Suzy and I were doing some work together for Parsons, so it was actually more convenient for her to have me close by. The house was a huge penthouse with wings, so we almost never crossed paths. I would go twice a year for two nights. I always brought Suzy and Chris a gift and took them out for dinner. I believe we all looked forward to the visits. But it's something else if the hosts don't have a mansion and the guests don't limit stays to two days.

I can hear people saying, "But what if I'm on a budget?" Then don't go!

I was talking about this book with my family and mentioned to my niece that she should show the book to her friend, who has done some pretty appalling things, in my opinion. My niece grew hysterical, literally, with the thought that her friend might be in the book.

Finally, I said, "If you think *she* is essential to this book, then this book is in trouble. Besides, why do you feel the need to defend her? How do you defend the fact that you filled the apartment with furniture from your family, and when you were away, she took half the living room furniture for her bedroom? Or that she borrowed your car and then crashed it? This is inappropriate behavior. Sorry, Wallace, she is now in the book!"

But I have the same hyperniceness Wallace has. When I lived in a studio in D.C., I would give my guests the foldout couch I usually slept on and I would sleep on the floor in the sleeping bag I kept in the closet. I didn't want my guest to be uncomfortable. If I'm going to be a host, I'm going to be a good host. And my new mantra is: If I can't handle it, I will just say so.

A friend from out of town e-mailed me recently and said he wanted to see my new apartment. I knew he was fishing for a place to stay, and after the initial flush of panic passed, I realized that I would actually like to see him and that I should invite him to stay. After all, I can't continue the rest of my life in fear of houseguests. I have to get myself unstuck.

Maybe the moral is that if you're the traveler and you don't have the financial resources to take care of yourself and to honor the host, then don't make the trip. But if you're the potential host, you should be honest about what you can and can't do, and then be as hospitable as possible—and no more.

RULE 11

Use Technology;
Don't Let It Use You

RECENTLY AT THE GROCERY store, the woman behind me had a mere carton of juice, and I had a whole cart full of items, so I said, "Please, go in front of me."

Did she even acknowledge this? She did not. Clearly she wasn't deaf, because she did, indeed, walk in front of me. I was tempted to take back my offer.

A woman sitting next to me on an airplane asked for the in-flight magazine. I handed it over with a smile. She didn't even look up or say anything at all. I was sorry I'd given it to her.

There should be a lot more thank-yous. I get irked every day when I hold the door for people and they don't say thank you.

And I'm starting to think that a lot of times it has to do with people being so in their own worlds. You see people walking through the world staring at their BlackBerries or iPhones. Doors are opening for them. Change is being made. People are making way. But they don't acknowledge it, because they're on that *thing*.

On several flights I've been on, the flight attendants have reached a point of exasperation, saying, "We can't leave until everything with an on/off button is turned off!" People aren't even processing that because they're so distracted by their gadgets. Or they're thinking, "My BlackBerry isn't going to take this plane down."

How important could the messages be? Is your wife having a baby this second? And if so, why are you on the plane? If you're on your way to her, how about just texting, "Be right there, honey," and then turning off the phone?

This kind of technological distraction is everywhere. At Dunkin' Donuts, the person behind the counter was saying, "Excuse me!" to the man who was first in line. He was on his phone, so he didn't even notice. The counter person went to the second person in line, and then suddenly the first guy said, "Hey!"

"Ah, you're out of your coma!" the person behind the counter said.

I feel like an old fart sometimes, but I wonder, Where does this take us? These sidewalks aren't designed for zombies, nor are our highways.

I hear there is a new application for iPhones that lets you see the sidewalk behind the phone while you text. That to me seems like surrender. You can't read e-mail while doing anything as complex as walking down a crowded sidewalk or driving on a highway.

It's impossible for your brain to take in that much information, at least it certainly is for me. Once when I was on *Today* in New York live via satellite from Los Angeles, I was looking directly into a camera that had Matt Lauer's interview questions for me on the screen. Since the words that appeared weren't mine, I wasn't supposed to read them, but they were so terribly distracting that I couldn't think straight. And all I had to do was chat. I didn't have to navigate a crowd or traffic!

It may seem crazy to stress manners when it can be hard enough just keeping it together day to day. When I flip through old etiquette books from the fifties and sixties, I see why people think talking about manners is ridiculous. In one old book, you have proclamations like:

"Boy's hands on wheel. Girl's hands at her side."

"Shorts are out of place on the street."

"Don't chew gum in church."

"Follow your hostess in putting your napkin in your lap."

"Choose congenial friends." It'd be nice if you knew in advance!

And then there are all of the etiquette book particulars about table settings. Mrs. Post, I don't even *own* fish forks!

But real etiquette helps. Sometimes it's practical, or it used to be. Traditionally, men walked on the outside of the sidewalk and women on the inside. I believe that goes back to the period in history when people threw their chamber pots from their windows onto the streets below. The person walking on the outside of the sidewalk would get hit, and better for it to be the man, who didn't have petticoats to wash.

In general, when it comes to etiquette, I don't care about all that fussy stuff regarding salad forks, but rather about the fundamentals of conscientious behavior. It's good for you and those around you, and it's good for preserving a social order that supports everyone. The key things are to be as thoughtful as possible of others and to pay attention to the messages you're sending out, and the means by which you're sending them.

When someone dies, it's good to mail a note. Don't send an e-mail. You have to send a card. Everyone should have cards and stamps kicking around. I have some very simple stationery, just nice card stock with my name at the top. You don't have to write a long note. I learned something from Diana Vreeland: What you write should be pithy and memorable. All people need to know is that you're thinking about them: "Thinking about you at this difficult time. I was so sorry to hear of your loss." Done.

When the news is happy, e-mail is fine. You can e-mail congratulations about babies, weddings, anything. But when it's not? If it's a death or other bad news, you have to be more formal.

I wasn't the only one who was a little horrified by Ashton Kutcher's reference to his former girlfriend Brittany Murphy's death. He wrote on Twitter: "2day the world lost a little piece of sunshine. My deepest condolences go out 2 Brittany's family, her husband, & her amazing mother Sharon."

People use texting and e-mail for everything, but it's not appropriate for somber situations. If you win an Oscar, tweet away, but if you're talking about a death or an illness, you need to use more formal channels. For example:

You can promote an employee via e-mail, but you can't fire him.

You can ask someone out by e-mail, but you can't break up with her.

Happy occasions can be casual. Sad or serious ones require a personal touch.

Fighting by e-mail is bad, too. I'm all for writing down the angry e-mail, but don't send it. That carefully crafted note never has the effect you want it to have. It just inflames the situation. Print it out and then delete it. Then you have the reference for the phone call or the meeting. It will save you a lot of stress and conflict. Every time I've blown up in a moment of frustration I've regretted it.

The worst was a few years ago when I sent an angry e-mail late at night to a TV executive. He'd called to yell at me about something I'd said to the press. I took the high road at the time and was contrite on the phone. But then I stewed about it all night. I thought: *How dare you?* And I started thinking counterproductive things like: *I could have said this much worse thing to the press!* I wrote it all down in an e-mail and rather than just saving it and cooling off, I hit send.

The next morning, I woke up with one thought: *I can't believe I sent that.*

I sent a new e-mail apologizing and called later and just said, "Sorry."

It blew over, and I learned that many mistakes can be undone. But I thought, *Never again.* When you take into account the emotional wear and tear, you realize it's better to let most sleeping dogs lie. I've learned at the age of fifty-seven that as much as I'd like to say X, Y, or Z, I must consider how I am going to feel afterward. And the answer, in the case of angry or snide remarks, is: not great.

I also learned about e-mail attachments the hard way. Someone sent me an e-mail when I was at Parsons with an attachment saying, "What kind of a jerk is this guy?" I wrote back, "He demonstrates every time he puts a word to paper that he's a complete and total asshole." I thought I was responding to her, but in fact I was responding to the guy. He had a good sense of humor about it, luckily, and wrote me back, saying, "I've been called worse." I was mortified.

And yet, I will say a misdirected e-mail saved my fiftieth birthday. My dear friends the Banus and a colleague at Parsons were planning a surprise party for me. Meanwhile, I was having a huge falling-out with the colleague at Parsons. There was a volley of e-mails about the details of the party, and someone cc'ed me by accident. Suddenly, I see the whole sequence of correspondence and learned that my mother was coming; my sister and her family were coming; I even think that the Queen of England was coming.

Furthermore, this was during the time when tumultuous curricular and pedagogical changes were taking place in the Fashion Design Department, and I was woefully unpopular with the faculty. They were invited, too. So I responded to this unintentional "cc" and called the whole thing off. Thank you, technology!

Things do happen for a reason. As terrible as I would have felt doing this to my friends, had I arrived at the Banus and been met with this surprise, I would have walked out. They were inviting people I was all but at war with, and I really doubt I could have played nice.

I am really against surprise parties, especially if they involve people from different spheres. Assumptions that are made by either group about who should be included are almost always wrong. There are a lot of people with whom I interact because I have to; that doesn't mean I want to eat cake with them. And then if they brought me a present, I would have to write a note.

One little technology-taming tip, If you, too, are surprised by typos: I like to print out things I'm working on to read them on paper before I send them off. You miss a lot of things on the screen that are apparent when you're looking at them on the page. Yes, there is the environment to think of, but—to paraphrase a certain celebrity on the topic of her fur coat being dead when she got it ("I didn't kill it!" she said)—the tree's already been taken down.

Don't Lose Your Sense of Smell

WHEN PRESENTED WITH BIZARRE circumstances—such as radical (and radically unappealing) cosmetic surgery—I'll mutter, "That person is living in the monkey house."

What does the phrase mean? I'm assuming that most readers have been to a monkey house at a zoo. The stench of it is like nothing I've ever experienced. Every time I visit, I can't help but declare, "This place stinks!" Well, after about ten or fifteen minutes, it no longer smells as bad. And after half an hour, it doesn't smell *at all*.

The trouble with that is the following: It still stinks. We're merely used to it, so the smell disappears to us. However, anyone walking into the monkey house anew is going to scream, "This place stinks!"

Once I bought a lamp, and the wrong color was delivered. It was pretty garish. But I was so desperate for light that I set it up. I thought: *That is horrible looking.* But as time went by, I grew used to it, and after a couple of weeks I even started to like it. I began to refer to its garish color as being "unexpected." Then a dear friend, an interior designer, came over to my apartment for a visit. She gasped when she saw the lamp and said, "What possessed you to get *that*?"

I'd been living in the monkey house.

You can tell when what you're doing is what you're meant to be doing. If it's fun, and satisfying, and comes together in a great way, then you know that's something you're in some way destined to do. If it feels dishonest, it probably is. While I think that it's good to step out of one's comfort zone and try new things, if in doing so, the particulars don't feel right, then they're not. That doesn't mean you shouldn't try new things, just that you should listen to yourself and learn from mistakes and not get so comfortable in a gross situation that you forget it smells.

So many people these days are switching jobs, or looking at new industries, and I think that, as tragic as the circumstances are, potential exists to try new things and find something truly fulfilling. But you really have to be flexible.

I see this all around me. We have been through meteoric adjustments at Liz Claiborne Inc., where I've been chief creative officer since 2007. Since the recession began, we've received completely new messages from the executive team. They are clear messages, but they require big changes. And yet I see so many associates failing to acknowledge that things have changed. The whole world has changed. And we need to adjust constantly.

We're going to need to rethink completely what we're doing in my own department at LCI. I actually really enjoy this kind of upheaval. I like the opportunity to evaluate what we do, and how we do it, and how we could do it better, or do it just as well with less. It's great to have the opportunity presented to us, because ordinarily we'd just keep slogging on in the same way. So many people I see complain when they're faced with changes, "But that's not the way we do things."

We *know* that. That's why we're having this discussion. Put it behind you.

It was like the curriculum development at Parsons. Whenever I would declare that we had to make changes, someone would say, "But this is the way we've always done it." I banned that phrase from my office. You just mustn't think that way. There is always room for improvement.

LCI's fabulous and inspirational CEO, Bill McComb, is always saying, "Don't look back." He's right. You can't bring all that baggage with you.

On my former Bravo show *Guide to Style,* I found people in a fashion rut with no clue how to get out of it. My job was to unwedge them from their rut, their own personal monkey house, and then to say, "You're out of the rut now. Where do you want to go? Who are you?"

The worst-case scenario is that it doesn't work and you go back to where you were before.

On Season 7 of *Runway,* I found with too much frequency that some of the designers would say, as early as ten p.m., that they were done and were going to surrender the remaining time.

"You're *done?*" I would ask them with a tone of shock. "If Leonardo had had more time with the *Mona Lisa,* it would be even more beautiful. Use the time and make it better."

There have always been designers on the show who wouldn't use the full time for whatever reason.

But never before Season 7 had I seen a whole group of people with such a languid approach to time. I call Season 7 the season of the sashay. No matter how close to the deadline they were, no matter how quickly they needed to get their models ready for the runway, there was no physical demonstration of urgency. Everyone just sashayed around the workroom and the sewing room.

Althea Harper was a little bit like this in Season 6. She was very last minute and would get caught up with the lichen on the bark; forget about the forest for the trees. "There's more to life than this ruched hem!" I would try to tell her.

In the same season, Johnny Sakalis and Mitchell Hall were social gadflies who just wanted to chat all the time. I said, "You two have work to do," and they would just keep gossiping. "We are late!" I'd be yelling at the workroom. "You need to move it!"

There they were, saying, "I'm coming . . . I just need to move *this* over *here* . . ." Slow as can be. All of them! A talented bunch of people, but wow, were they lackadaisical.

JUDGING ON *Project Runway* is sometimes about informing people that they are living in the monkey house. Often a designer has worked on something so long that he or she thinks it is the most beautiful garment on the face of the earth, when in fact it is an abomination.

Michael Kors is a great judge, and I think it's partly because he does such clean, elegant work that he has a great ability to let the designers be themselves and not project his own taste onto them. (Friends of mine who love to wear lavish jewelry are big fans of Michael Kors dresses, because his clothes have such simplicity that they make a fantastic frame for baubles.)

He and Nina Garcia play so well off each other, because they both have a great eye, and they aren't afraid to say what they think. There's a great exchange in Season 7 when Nina throws her arms up about a neckline treatment.

Michael says, "Nina! How many necklines do you ever really see? I can count them on one hand!" The two of them have a big debate about how much innovation is possible when it comes to necklines. *The Fairchild Dictionary of Fashion* (my bible!) devotes ten pages to necklines and collars, but the truth is that clothes today typically feature only a few different ones.

I love these kinds of specific conversations about fashion. It really gets at the heart of these choices the designers have to make, and it's so satisfying to listen in on these two important fashion people talking about it. Their squabbles are very instructive when it comes to how the design world approaches a burning issue like the boat neck.

It's a lot harder than it looks to be a judge. And when we have designers as guest judges, it's often hard for them to keep their own aesthetics in check. Most designers are incapable of understanding any aesthetic other than their own, and they want to impose it on the designers. Unlike most designer judges, Michael is really terrific about seeing each designer on his or her own merits. It's a rarity.

Nina has a great eye, but there was one time she championed a dress that everyone else hated, and that I would say belonged in the monkey house. Perhaps you'll recall the green neoprene dress Ra'mon Lawrence Coleman made in Season 6. He was dyeing it in the toilet before I suggested he take pity on the model who had to wear it and switch to the sink. The dress, a hot green mess thrown together at the last minute, was a disaster.

Well, Nina had a forty-five-minute filibuster for the neoprene dress. Nina is so tough and cool that she has the capacity to intimidate Heidi (and all of us a bit, truth be told). Nina's trump card was her crystal-clear assertion that she would wear the dress. With that said, Heidi went along with it, too. Well, the look I thought was going to send Ra'mon home ended up winning the challenge for him. I couldn't believe it.

Project Runway auctions the winning looks of each season, so I bought the dress for Nina. It went for $305. When it arrived in a little cardboard box, I couldn't believe how tiny it was, just two pieces of neoprene sort of glommed together. Seeing it up close was very illuminating. There were yellow pins sticking out of it, rough edges, spattered dye—and I still haven't figured out how to assemble the top. Thank goodness I won it rather than some fan, who would have gotten that package and declared, "This *won?*"

I'm planning to send it to Nina with the suggestion that she wear it for the next event we have to do together. I have a feeling she won't.

In any case, what keeps the show from turning into one big monkey house is the seriousness with which our judges take the matter of construction and design. During the runway show there is a huge amount of deliberation, far more than most people realize. From the moment that the judges see the work on the runway to the moment Heidi says who's in and out, five to six hours elapse, not the several minutes you see at home.

I'm frequently wrong not just about who will be chosen as the winner, but also about who's in the top or bottom three. Sometimes it flips while they're deliberating. The judges change their minds a lot before they reach a verdict, which I believe is positive and a great testament to the seriousness of their discussion.

Guest judges are real wild cards when it comes to what they like. Sometimes a guest judge will say, "This was my favorite look!" And all the others had it as something that justified sending someone home. That's why Heidi rarely asks the guest judge to speak first anymore. In the make-each-other-over challenge in Season 2, Santino Rice's jumpsuit for Kara Janx might well have sent him home had Freddie Leiba not said right off the bat that he loved that look.

It's all edited out in the final show, but one guest judge told the designers what she would have done had she been designing for the challenge. "I would have picked this fabric, instead! I would have designed it this way!"

That is not helpful. The competing designers didn't use that fabric or that silhouette, so how can you judge them on what you would have done rather than on what they did in fact do?

In the finale of Season 3, Nina Garcia, not I, was scheduled to give the designers a critique early in the week. But because of the whole Is-Jeffrey-cheating debacle, she came in late on Thursday, instead. The Bryant Park fashion show was going to be held the following morning.

When I arrived after the critique, I asked the producers, "How did it go?" and they said Nina had given the designers a hard time. I was disappointed to hear that, because I thought, *What are they going to do? The show is tomorrow. At this point in the game, negativity isn't helpful.*

So I did my routine for the camera, and then I went back to the designers and said, "I heard the visit was hard." Everyone shrugged. Laura Bennett looked up and wisely said, "As if we could do anything! We didn't even listen."

She was correct. Sometimes it's just too late to rethink and rework, even if the advice is brilliant.

Which brings us back to something I keep finding myself saying in this book: Context is everything—for clothes, for behavior, and for expectations. Truth telling is good, but you also have to accept the conditions as they are.

When someone is about to head onstage or on camera, do you tell her she has parsley in her teeth? Absolutely. That is helpful. But do you say, "That is a terrible dress"?

No! There's no time to change, and she'll just go out there feeling bad about herself. Similarly, I stop making comments, especially comments that suggest that an item should be reworked, the day before Bryant Park, because negative notes aren't helpful at that point, unless you're addressing matters of accessories or styling or the looks' order on the runway. To suggest starting over is no longer feasible.

The question I ask myself before giving advice is: Is what you want to say really going to help them?

Sometimes it's very clear. For example, recently I was doing an interview on camera. The interviewer's lapel was sticking up, and I could tell it wasn't just a jaunty affectation, so I said, "Before we start, let me fix this," and I adjusted his collar.

"Thank you!" he said, rather relieved.

"I'd want you to do the same for me!" I said.

If you're getting dressed with a friend, you can say, "You should rethink those shoes." But you need to have supplies available! When Leah Salak, a colleague of mine at Liz Claiborne Inc., and I do shopping mall events together, and she asks, "How do I look?" I take the question seriously. People are videotaping these events, and there are thousands of people in attendance. I don't want her to regret anything later. And we have a ton of options around here at the office, so I can say, "That cut's not quite right for you. Let's see what else we have." Then we can pick out something truly gorgeous.

Also, I give her advice because—and this is an important distinction—she *asked*. If someone doesn't ask, you don't have a moral obligation to say every thought that pops into your head. As I've mentioned, strangers are constantly saying to me, "I was so afraid of what you would say about what I'm wearing!"

As if I just go around analyzing the outfits of everyone I pass on the street! Certainly not. I never say anything unless I'm asked, and then if I'm asked, I consider the matter carefully and offer an honest opinion.

I try to phrase criticism in the nicest possible way, but I also never lie. If people ask, I assume it's because they want to know. People are not dumb about these things; they can tell when a compliment isn't sincere.

My grandmother had the most backhanded way of delivering compliments. She was always saying things like, "You look so much better than you did the last time I saw you."

What in the world does she mean? we were always wondering. *What did I look like the last time?* Her compliments always left us confused rather than proud.

WHEN YOU PUT YOURSELF out there, whether it's by delivering a speech, acting in a play, or putting out a collection, you want feedback that's positive, or at the very least helpful for the next time.

If you want to stay friends with people who put themselves out in this way, it's often necessary to deliver vague praise that doesn't actually address the specifics of the production. Examples include: "Congratulations!" or "That was quite a performance!" or "I'll never forget that!" or the classic: "Oh, *you*!"

I find myself in the position of delivering a lot of these euphemisms. My favorite is "That was unforgettable!" For the right reasons? (Pause.) Repeat: "That was unforgettable!"

IT'S VERY IMPORTANT TO be totally honest when it comes to things that can be changed and that must be changed. As you know, I am passionate about education. When you expect a lot out of children, they will rise to the occasion. Education is so important, and I love when I see children at a school that's right for them. Having a great teacher can change a child's life. And while I know how busy parents are today, I love seeing families doing their best to support their schools and work as partners with their children's teachers.

"Make it work" applies to all areas of life. If there's something you hate about your school, or your neighborhood, or your child's sports team, make it work! Get involved in the PTA, contact your representatives in the government, or offer to assistant coach.

Too many of the parents I dealt with in higher education seemed to feel that they had to start a fight to get what they wanted. As the chair of the Fashion Design Department, I was the enemy. If the students didn't have top-of-the-line resources or materials, it had to be my fault. Well, I was working incredibly hard to improve those things and was making great strides, but with no help, things take a while. What I always loved to hear was, "We need to get the students X, Y, and Z. What help do you need to make that happen?"

It wasn't like I didn't know. Frequently, I would disarm students and parents by saying, "You're right. There is a problem there." There is no reason to try to hide things; it doesn't work! I could tell the complainers, "We need this amount of money added to our budget in this area," or "We need a contact at this organization to get this grant." If others besides me were advocating for something, it tended to happen much faster than it otherwise would have.

They would expect me to be defensive, but I would say, "You're right. We need to fix that. Here's why we haven't fixed it so far, and here's our plan to get it done."

It gets a little trickier when you start talking about faculty. I couldn't really say, "You're right. She's a lousy teacher." It used to be that you could say, "This isn't working out," and let someone go. But when a faculty union arrived at Parsons, I couldn't even use those sobering words, because I was "threatening" them. I asked, "Who are we serving? Answer: the students. If they're being disadvantaged by a teacher's failings, we're at fault."

Furthermore, under the new union guidelines, once a teacher had been there for a while, it was all but impossible to dismiss her.

I had one teacher who was a real problem and who was approaching the deadline after which we couldn't let him go without a great deal of work. So I spoke to the Legal Department and I spoke with HR, and we were all in agreement that I could do the deed after the semester's grades were posted. We had meetings. We were all set to go. And then both departments backed down. I said, "This appointment shouldn't have been made to begin with, and I made it. I regret my mistake. Now we have an opportunity to get out of it, and you won't stand by me?" I had a responsibility to the students. Ironically but thankfully, I left a month later to join Liz Claiborne Inc.

When I used to give tours of Parsons, it was a real dump. I would proudly talk about all the positive aspects of the school and would avoid mentioning the poor facilities. With some frequency, parents would say, "This places looks . . . crummy."

Antagonistic tour takers would make me crazy. Sometimes they'd be especially rude, and I always thought, *What if your kid winds up going to this school? He's going to be the Son of That Jerk from the Tour.*

But the ones who asked why the building looked so bad had a point. For a long time, I would try to ignore it, like that W. C. Fields line, "Get away from me, kid, you're bothering me."

Finally, I realized I had to address it, so I turned it into a joke. I would say, "I'm sure you've noticed the state of our building. Well, this didn't happen overnight. It took years and years—and *years*—for us to get it to look this way. Ha-ha."

It didn't lessen the amount of peeling paint, but at least people would laugh. And it gets directly to my point about the monkey house. If you're going to live in one, you at least have to keep reminding yourself that it still does stink!

Know What to Get Off Your Chest and What to Take to the Grave

G ET IT OFF YOUR chest" is one of the all-time worst cli-
chés. If you have done something shameful, the logic
goes, you should confess and be forgiven.

Hold it right there. Think about it. Would revealing your
mistake hurt others? If so, then hold your tongue. It may make
you feel better to tell someone you've cheated on him, for example, but it makes the other person feel miserable. That's not
fair. He did nothing wrong, and yet he has to suffer while you
get to feel cleansed.

I know a woman who said of her husband: "If he cheated
on me, I would hope he had the maturity to keep it to himself.
Let him suffer with the secret. It's his penance for doing what
he did."

I'm with her. You hear people say, "I'll feel better if I tell my
spouse I was unfaithful." Of course *you* will. But maybe you're
not supposed to feel better.

On one *Project Runway* home visit, I was struck by how
the designer's parents' divorce was still weighing on her. Her
mother and father had been separated for years and years and

came together for the occasion of this home visit to celebrate their daughter's success.

I thought that was lovely, but I also felt so sorry for the designer's mother. She was reminding her daughter of what her father had done, and you could tell she was still suffering years after the fact. Then the father walked in, happy-go-lucky and carefree. Clearly, when he revealed to his wife that he was a cad, he felt purged and had his catharsis. Meanwhile, his wife was destroyed by it.

That's why "getting it off your chest" isn't necessarily a good idea.

As you probably know, if you are familiar with any recovering addicts, those in twelve-step programs like Alcoholics Anonymous typically try to make amends to those whom they have hurt. But in my experience some people don't pay attention to the second part of the step: "Make direct amends to such people wherever possible, *except when to do so would injure them or others.*"

I know someone who received an amends call that informed her that her friend had stolen from her for years. The friend said, "Sorry!" And that was the end of the amends.

Well, not good enough. My friend was furious, while the thief felt totally relieved that she'd unburdened herself of this secret. Who was really served by this? The victim had to suffer more, and the perpetrator was vindicated. If the apology had to happen, it should have been followed up with a great big check to make up for all that had been stolen.

When you're thinking of volunteering advice, you also need to ask yourself this question: Will revealing my feelings on this subject actually help?

My friend Richard Thomas was in David Mamet's play

Race on Broadway, and one night in 2009 Anna Wintour was in the audience. Richard called his teenage son, Montana, who is obsessed with fashion, and said, "Anna Wintour's here! You should come over."

"I'm afraid," the boy said to his father.

He had reason to be. Anna took Richard aside after the show and said, "I have a note for you about your performance. You're dressing very poorly. You need a much more expensive suit."

The suit was Prada. How much more expensive does it get? I can't believe that a costumer, a director, and all these other people would let an actor out onstage in a starring role if he didn't look great. She apparently couldn't help herself from expressing an opinion. In a case like this, if you have a criticism, you really should keep it to yourself.

This question of what to say or not to say is a running theme in my family. One tense holiday season, we had a family conversation about what we could do to have a better time together.

"We could all say a lot less," I suggested. "Everyone in this family shares *entirely too much*. Before speaking, let's ask ourselves if this is something people really need to know."

As I anticipated, the Gunns nixed my strategy.

There was one night when we were visiting my mother and all hell was breaking loose. She was going after my sister about the inevitability of some problems my sister was having with her son. "I spotted it at a very early age," my mother bragged.

Not even *remotely* helpful. It just pushed a button in my sister that caused her to lose it. She was sobbing and ran out of the room.

"Was that really necessary?" I asked my mother. "You took

a nice little gathering in your hospital room and turned it into *The Jerry Springer Show.*

"Besides," I asked her, "why not say something when the situation is actually fixable rather than years later when the damage has been done?"

"I don't butt in," she replied.

Translation: *When it's fixable, I don't say anything. I wait until it's done, and then remind you about it.* If you're so sure at the time, do an intervention. Otherwise, you should keep your mouth shut forever after.

This is my whole way of operating on *Project Runway.* After the judging, we're back in the lounge and sometimes a designer will tell me, "Nina and Heidi were telling me how bad this aspect of the garment was, and you never mentioned it."

"And I never would," I say, "because you couldn't have done anything about that particular aspect of your design."

At the same time, some secrets shouldn't be kept. A friend whom I love and adore was diagnosed years ago with a degenerative disease. Somehow, her husband learned about it before she did and kept it from her for some two or three years, until her symptoms were evident to her.

When my friend told me this story, she suggested that this was a tremendously generous and romantic gesture on her husband's part.

"I hate to respond this way," I replied, "but I'm not even remotely moved by this story. It makes me angry."

"Why?" she asked, shocked.

"What if your last wish were to climb to the top of an Aztec pyramid or to rappel down the side of the Empire State Building?" I asked. "What if? You would have had three years to do those things before your illness progressed."

Plus, I found it infantilizing. My friend is a very strong, very smart woman. Her husband thought the diagnosis would weigh on her, and so he thought it was good that she didn't know, but I maintain it wasn't his call.

Still, I know that some of her friends think how wonderful it was of her husband to keep this secret from her for years.

"He wanted to protect you from this," they say to her, all moony.

Protect her? It was going to happen anyway!

I guess if she's happy he kept the secret, then he made the right choice, but I still have trouble with that story. Maybe it's just that it pains me to see people being lied to "for their own good."

Maybe I'm just extra defensive because I was lied to by a man for many years and still haven't fully gotten over it. I've had only one long-term relationship in my adult life. In my twenties, I was madly, passionately, unconditionally in love with the same man for almost a decade. It was fabulous, I thought, but I was living in a fool's paradise. What's the opposite of a monkey house, where everything smells pristine and is not? Maybe it's just another room in the monkey house.

We were together for nine years and more or less living with each other, but I still had my apartment. We worked together, so I saw him every day and night. One night we were in bed watching *M*A*S*H*. He turned to me and said, "I don't have the patience for you any longer."

"What?" I responded. "What am I doing? What can I do?"

"There's nothing for you to do," he said. "I want you to leave."

Then he told me that he'd been sleeping around—with any guy, anywhere. And of course this was during the advent of AIDS, 1982. So not only was he throwing me out abruptly after I'd spent almost my whole adult life with him, but he was revealing to me that a major part of our relationship had been a sham, and that he'd put my very life at risk.

I still remember driving down Rock Creek Parkway back to my apartment that night. I had to pull over because I was hyperventilating. I could hardly breathe from grief, humiliation, and despair. Those feelings later turned to anger.

His moral behavior was horrible, but he also put my health in real jeopardy. I was monogamous. I was in love, why wouldn't I be? I never thought he wouldn't be. To find out he'd been cheating for years was such a slap in the face and also potentially a death sentence. I was tested for HIV every six months for years. Thank God, I was okay, but I've never quite learned to trust anyone intimately again.

And then I still had to see him at work every day. It was no fun being in academic meetings with the person who'd broken my heart. I took the high road. But it was not easy. Doing the right thing can be very, very hard, and I think it was also the right thing that I left town as soon as I could. I moved to New York City the following year, and this breakup was most certainly a catalyst.

When people hear that I haven't had a boyfriend since 1982, they often whisper, "Does he not have sex?"

That's right!

You know, much of my one long-term boyfriend's "I'm over this" was about not having the patience for me with regard to sex. I've always been kind of asexual. So now I can't even consider sex without thinking about him and his disapproval. Talk about something that will make you lose the urge. That breakup was a cold shower to last a lifetime.

Could I get psychiatric help and resume some kind of sex life at some point? Probably. But it's a little late for that. And frankly, I am happy being celibate. That doesn't mean I haven't had thoughts. I am a human being. But I love my life and don't feel any need to change it.

Getting used to being alone was hard, but now that I've made a life for myself alone, I really like it. It's been years since I've been interested in anyone. And I really think if you don't need it, you don't need it. As hard as it is for a lot of my friends to believe, I really am happy alone.

Okay, there has been one man I've had feelings for since then. When I was traveling to Asia regularly, I often had the same flight attendant, a man named Daniel. He was very cute and very kind, and I always looked forward to seeing him. Well, on one flight, a baby broker boarded the plane with—I kid you not—fourteen Asian babies bound for America. It would never happen now. But there were the fourteen babies, and something had to be done, because this broker was completely outnumbered and overwhelmed, as you may imagine.

So a flight attendant got on the intercom and asked for volunteers to take a baby for the international flight. I didn't have much work to do, so I held my hand up and was assigned an adorable baby boy. For fourteen hours, he sat on my lap and ripped up magazines. I made faces at him, and he slept, and it was perfectly lovely.

Well, I guess this babysitting marathon impressed Daniel, because when we landed in New York, he said, "Would you mind if I called you?"

I said that would be great, and he did, and we went out and had a wonderful time. We started seeing each other whenever he was in town. About two months in, I started to think, *This could be something.* I really liked him and he had a lot to recommend him: He was my age. He traveled a lot. And he had almost no *stuff.* (This was key because I was nowhere near ready to merge households with anyone.) I was, for the first time since my horrible breakup, really and truly happy about being in a relationship.

Well, I made the foolish mistake of sharing my happiness with a colleague whom I trusted.

When I told him about Daniel, he had no reason to wish me anything but congratulations. We weren't lovers. He had a partner of many years. But he went crazy and called me a fool.

"A flight attendant?" he spluttered. "What a stereotype!"

"Your boyfriend's a *florist!*" I said, furious. "You don't call a fashion designer and a florist being together a stereotype?"

We had a big falling-out over it. But he succeeded in shaking my very fragile faith in this new relationship. At least indirectly, it caused me to say good-bye to Daniel.

This was eighteen years ago. Sometimes I wonder whatever happened to Daniel. He was a really good man, and I'm sure he's made a good life for himself, unlike my former friend, who now lives in a town called Crossville. I think it's a good place for him, because he is still constantly cross!

You know people like this, right? People who are incapable of enjoying anything? I'll never forget the time when someone I know ruined the rehearsal dinner of his dear friend's daughter by throwing a fit because she hadn't had him make her bridal gown. He went on and on. By the end of his litany, his friend was sobbing. It was so painful and horrible. He was mad that the wedding wasn't about him.

Have you noticed how depressed people seem to show up at memorial services? Maybe it's because they want to show that they're still here. Or maybe they can get behind an unhappy event because there everyone feels the way they do every day.

Some people walk around under a rain cloud of their own making. In my encounters with Narciso Rodriguez and Isabel Toledo I've always found them a bit sulky, but at least they make sulking look glamorous, and they can express joy when need be. "The world is a beautiful place," gloomy Narciso effuses in a cheerful print advertisement for a cell phone. "Liar, liar, pants on fire!" I shouted at the magazine page. But I am impressed that he was able to crack such a big smile.

So there's a secret that should be hidden: unbridled pessimism. If you think the world is terrible or that someone shouldn't be so happy with a flight attendant or in any other situation, keep it to yourself.

Then again, you need to be true to yourself, and for me that means not being coy about my sexuality. One thing that causes me to well up with emotion is when young men come up to me and say that I've helped them handle their sexuality; that is, coming to terms with being gay. It reminds me how lonely I was as a child with no gay role models.

Everyone needs a role model to look up to. When I was young and thinking I might not be John Wayne material, all I had for a role model was Paul Lynde from *Bewitched*. You may remember him as one of the more insane people on *Hollywood Squares*? Well, he was completely gawky and ridiculous on screen, and then in 1965, his boyfriend fell out a hotel window and died. (They may have had a few drinks.)

So that's what I felt I had to look forward to as a gay man: playing ridiculed characters and having a tragic personal life. The gay people in the popular imagination back then were all predators or weirdos. Meanwhile, my straight friends had Clark Gable, Tony Curtis, Charlton Heston, and a million other heartthrobs to look up to. (A lot of famous fifties actors were later revealed to be gay; if only I'd known at the time!)

I often say in keynote addresses to college students that I figured out what I wasn't before I figured out what I was. That struggle to find out who you are is so hard. You have to keep eliminating things that you aren't and then see what's left over. Most important, you should never pretend. There's nothing harder than living life as someone you're not, even if being what you are is very hard, which is what being gay was for me for a very long time.

One of the few times my father was physically violent with me was the evening we were to meet my grandfather's new wife. They were coming to our house. That afternoon, I was putting together my sister's Barbie & Ken Little Theatre ("After the show everything folds neatly away until the next performance!").

My father saw me playing around with these dolls in what I can only imagine was an effeminate way, and he started smacking me with a wet washcloth. "You're not going to be seen doing this!" he yelled at me.

It was terrifying, and I had no idea what I'd done to make him so mad or why it would be so awful if these people saw me with Barbie's theater. In retrospect, I can see he thought I was heading down a less-than-macho path, and he was hoping to beat it out of me. Well, sorry, Dad—didn't work!

When I told a friend of mine this story recently, she said, "Do you think maybe your father was secretly gay and disturbed by it?"

It has definitely occurred to me. He certainly did protest too much about those Barbies . . .

"And you don't think he and J. Edgar Hoover were an item, do you?" she added.

Well, let me tell you, I've been there.

I have no proof, and I'm going to say right now, my mother would deny it up and down, and so, probably, would many biographers of Hoover; I'm likely just totally wrong about this. But . . . The men were incredibly close. They were both arguably repressed. So even if they were sleeping together, you can bet they never would have admitted it, even to themselves. He would have really beaten it back. He certainly wanted to knock it out of me, literally and figuratively!

I don't believe my father ever had an affair. He was very respectful. He may never even have been tempted. He had strong moral fiber, and I can't believe he would have betrayed my mother. But I do think it's very possible that he was a big closet case.

I've always thought there was a touch of lavender in that bureau. There certainly were some issues. Of my father's close circle of work colleagues, every one of the men committed suicide by gunshot after retiring. In two out of four, it was to the head; the other two were to the chest. Talk about an angry, horrible way to die; there's a big mess to clean up. Dad was the only one who died a natural death. And from what I could tell, all the wives, aside from my mother, were barely functioning alcoholics.

I remember dinner parties at our house where the next morning you'd find people on the lawn. They would all get completely wasted. My father was a great enabler. He didn't drink wine—I think he thought that was too fey—but he drank everything else: scotch, vodka, beer, whatever. He spent the parties behind our bar, always filling glasses. He never let a glass be empty, even if you protested. This behavior was either extremely generous or completely crazy.

Lately, I've been thinking more about men of that era, specifically my father and his colleagues. Last week I was on the plane from Los Angeles to Portland, on a little plane and in first class, which was a nice change of pace. The guy next to me was Ron Howard's business partner, Brian Grazer. He was with a woman I didn't recognize, and they were talking movies. Specifically, they were talking about a biopic of Hoover.

It was hard, but I kept my mouth shut. I knew that I held within me some deeply personal stuff, and I didn't really want to tell these stories to a plane full of people I didn't know. Still, I did keep thinking: *Boy, could I fill in a lot of blanks for them.*

My father was an FBI special agent for twenty-six years and then retired and ran the Washington Bureau of *Reader's Digest* for ten years. As you'll recall, he was J. Edgar Hoover's ghostwriter. He wrote his books and speeches and traveled with Hoover.

J. Edgar Hoover: Now there was an interesting figure, to say the least. He was the director of the FBI from 1924 to 1972. I did go to Hoover's house occasionally. He had the only Astroturf lawn I knew of in all of Washington—I believe so he wouldn't have to have a gardener. He was very afraid of being spied on.

As most people now know, there have long been rumors that Hoover was a cross-dresser and gay, and that he was possibly having an affair with his deputy, Clyde Tolson. Hoover did surround himself with a lot of very handsome men, but

I wonder whether or not he was capable of having gay affairs without anyone knowing.

The rumors came out full force after my father was sick with Alzheimer's disease, and thank God, because my father was a very macho guy and would have been outraged. He supported Hoover unconditionally. He would have said it was a left-wing conspiracy.

But one thing happened that made me wonder if maybe he did know something about Hoover's supposed love of dresses and wigs. My sister and I used to take the FBI tour once a year. It was a big deal in D.C., and we never missed it. One year, 1961, when I was eight, I was on the tour and my father asked me if I'd like to meet Vivian Vance. According to Helen Gandy, Hoover's secretary, Vance was visiting Hoover, and she said she'd be happy to meet us.

I was a rabid *I Love Lucy* fan and was beside myself with excitement.

"Ethel Mertz is here?" I screamed. My father smiled and took my sister and me into Hoover's office, where I shook Vivian Vance's hand and chatted with her. I was thrilled.

Years later, I was reminiscing with my sister about the meeting, and suddenly I realized something. "Does it seem odd to you," I asked her, "that when we met Vivian Vance in Hoover's office, Hoover wasn't there?"

I've since looked at photos of both Hoover and Vivian Vance from that period of time, and the similarities are rather eerie . . .

I've called some Vivian Vance experts, including Rob Edelman and Audrey Kupferberg, who wrote *Meet the Mertzes: The Life Stories of I Love Lucy's Other Couple;* none of them knew of any meeting between Vance and Hoover.

I'm not saying at the age of eight I definitely met J. Edgar Hoover at his office in the FBI wearing a dress and makeup, only that I *strongly suspect* it. My mother says I'm crazy, but she wasn't there.

ANYWAY, THIS WOMAN ON the plane kept talking about Helen Gandy, Hoover's personal secretary, and how important she was to him. And yet, she never once mentioned Clyde Tolson, the associate director of the FBI with whom Hoover had lunch and dinner every day and traveled constantly. Tolson inherited Hoover's estate, and they're buried side by side.

She leaned over to me at one point and said, "I'll trade you my *New York Times* for your *Vanity Fair*. I thought she meant for the flight, but no, she meant for keeps. I saw her read an article about the military contractor and Blackwater founder Erik Prince and then put it into the flap in the back of the seat. I thought: *Give it back to me!*

Anyway, a few minutes later she started saying, "Let's do a biopic of Erik Prince!" She said it as if she was free associating.

And I thought: *Wow, you are shameless! I just read that same article. I could contribute more to this one than to the Hoover one!*

But: Take the high road, right? I bought another *Vanity Fair* at the terminal. It's not worth five dollars to get into a scrap.

Let that be a lesson, though. Who knows what kind of amazing stories she could have gotten out of me if, instead of swiping my magazine, she'd just offered me her paper and started up a friendly conversation?

Not that I love chatting on airplanes, or ever. I do like to keep to myself, a fact that drives my family insane. My mother in particular is incredibly outgoing. She doesn't believe anyone else should have secrets from her, ever. She's the kind of person who runs her gloved finger along the top of a picture frame to see if there's dust on it. I think that's ridiculous. Who cares if there's dust up there? If the house is a mess, let's talk about the dust that's down here on the table.

When my sister was living in Pottstown, Pennsylvania, my mother and I were visiting once, and as usual Mother was snooping. She went up into the attic, which was a bedroom, poked around, and came down to the first floor to tell me to go up there.

"Why would I do that?" I asked.

"To see how horrible it is," she said.

"I don't want to!" I said. "I wasn't invited."

"I want you to see it!" she insisted.

"I don't want to see it!" I insisted back.

This is the kind of thing we fight about: whether or not to go into my sister's attic to look at dust. I am all for people getting to keep private rooms private. Not so my mother. In fact, her snooping is such that she thought nothing of breaching national security.

After the tragic assassination of John F. Kennedy, the Warren Commission put together its famous report of what happened. Well, my father had an early, top-secret copy. He brought it home with him from work one night and, knowing my mother was eager to peek at it, hid it well—or so he thought.

My mother found it and locked herself in the bathroom so she could read it in peace. My father banged away at the door, but she wouldn't open it. Finally, my father took the door down with an axe. You'd think that would be enough to convince my mother to let secrets stay secret, but no, she's still just as snoopy as ever.

When it comes to what to conceal or what to reveal, I err on the side of privacy but also honesty, as you may have guessed by now.

I think it's best never to lie, because when you tell lies, you have to remember them. It makes life really complicated. I always tell the truth. It gets me in trouble sometimes, but at least I don't have to keep track of a whole bunch of crazy stories—at least not crazy ones that are made up!

When in Rome . . .
I Still Wouldn't Eat Monkey Brains

M Y FAMILY IS ORIGINALLY Norwegian. We were thrown out of Norway in the ninth century and wound up in Scotland. Our coat of arms says, "Make peace, not war." It may as well have said, "No live food, please," for we are a timid people when it comes to eating, and my extensive business travels through Asia have definitely challenged my constitution, and my sense that what constitutes good manners must be universal.

For example, one doesn't firmly shake hands in Malaysia. Traditionally, you put both your hands out and then touch your heart. And invites aren't always real. I was asked to someone's home in Malaysia and said, "Yes!" Well, the person asking me was deadpan. He walked away without saying anything else. The people I was with said, "You have to say 'no' the first two times you're asked, and then you say 'yes' the third time." I wasn't actually invited to dinner! It was just the first ask.

It's important to do research if you're going to another country, especially if you're doing business there. You have a responsibility to know the ways of the culture. What if someone from Malaysia comes here? Should they shake our hands? I think generally it's good to practice house rules, to make an effort to adopt local customs. But it's also good to be flexible when it comes to our expectations of people from abroad.

When it comes to food, I never want to be an ugly American, but I also don't want to end up in a hospital, if only for psychological reasons. I've had some very disquieting food experiences, and they have seriously tested my ability to be a gracious guest. Let me tell you a little about how I wound up in Korea and Japan, and then I'll tell you about things crawling off my plate.

Parsons developed academic options abroad called Two Plus Two Affiliate Programs, whereby students would spend two years at a Parsons affiliate abroad followed by two years at Parsons in New York. I was flying somewhere in Asia once a month for eight years, and for example, I was not permitted to visit Seoul, South Korea, and Kanazawa, Japan, on the same trip, because culturally it would be insulting to each party to reveal that you were traveling for any business other than theirs. You'd like to think you could just pretend you'd arrived fresh from New York City, but they would find out. I learned a great deal about homage and ego in these cultures.

And the food did occasionally scare me. At one dinner in Korea at a Japanese restaurant called the Great Wall, a plate came out with something on it that looked like a big Tootsie Roll. I was looking at it and waiting for everyone to be served before beginning. And as I was contemplating it, it started to squirm its way off the plate. It was a live sea slug.

I waited for it to squirm completely off the plate and reach the table. Then I put my plate on top of it and casually leaned on it. If I was even going to think about eating it, I had to kill it first. But then I realized I could leave it under there, and it would look like I'd cleaned my plate. The person who came to clear noticed the flattened slug under my plate, but he politely picked it up and carried it off.

My general rule of thumb is that if it's alive, it shouldn't be any bigger than an oyster. And it should not have eyes. And it shouldn't be able to walk off your plate under its own steam.

When I was in Kanazawa, I took a stroll in the seafood market and couldn't believe how expensive everything was. I saw a $5,000 crab! The dean of Parsons and I were taken to a seafood meal by a group of businessmen who were part of the Chamber of Commerce. There was a man-made stream running through the restaurant and an aquarium by the entrance full of tiny goldfish. While we were waiting, people on line were reaching into the aquarium and popping these little fish in their mouths—like Pepperidge Farm Goldfish, only alive.

At the table, a whole fish was presented to us ceremoniously. The waiter took what looked like an eye-drop bottle that we're told was filled with sake. He dropped a little into the fish's mouth, and the fish, which was flayed, mind you, started to writhe. I was horrified, but I did have one happy thought. I leaned over to my colleague and said, "Remember when you were asked yesterday if you'd rather go to the seafood restaurant or the beef restaurant? Thank you for saying the seafood one. Can you imagine what they'd do to a cow?"

The bill was $7,000 for six of us. Evidently in the Japanese culture people live modestly except when it comes to going out. Torturing fish with sake drops isn't cheap.

But it brings up an important question: How polite does

one have to be? After bearing witness to its torment, I couldn't eat the fish. Fortunately, in the Asian culture there are usually several courses, so you can bow out of the ones that scare you and say, "Thank you, but I think I will save myself for the next atrocity."

For the record, I know people eat insects in certain cultures, and I am much more okay with that than with the writhing live animals. I'll go with a bug over a mammal any day. At least they don't look you in the eye.

Also, for the record, I'm not against eating animals. I wear leather and I eat meat, but I draw the line at inhumane fur. I've worked with PETA to help educate the public about it. I say, know where your food comes from, and take responsibility for it. I'm no zealot; I just think we should be as humane as possible, and when it comes to fur, there are alternatives.

I got involved with PETA because Parsons was inviting the International Fur Trade Federation to speak, and I thought the students needed to hear the other side. I don't think fur is always bad. I visited a Saga Furs of Scandinavia fur farm in Denmark, where they raise fox and mink in an ethical way. I always say, if you absolutely must have a fur, make sure Saga is the fur source. They have bred the animals' natural instincts out of them over time so their foxes and minks are basically domesticated and have a very happy life before they become stoles.

I really do understand vegetarianism, even though I'm a failure at it.

In college I was so traumatized by the slaughterhouse scene in James Agee's short story "A Mother's Tale" that I became an instant vegetarian. I swore off meat. It repulsed me.

Then, several months later, I was feeling weak, and a voice from within said, "I need meat! I need it immediately!"

I went to the local grocery store, ran to the packaged meat section, grabbed a package of bologna, and ate the whole thing standing there in the aisle. Then I paid for the empty container. I proudly help PETA with their antifur campaign, but they know they're not going to make a vegan out of me. And yet they still named me their 2009 Man of the Year (Ellen DeGeneres was their Woman of the Year) because of my crusade against abuse in the fur trade.

Vegetarianism can make for social awkwardness at times, especially if you're at an event where only hunks of meat are served. You may think this is rare, but vegetarian friends tell me that it does happen. In those situations it really is a question of just eating enough not to insult the host.

One person I know was at a fancy luncheon at which they were serving venison and nothing else. There was no way to get around it, so he ate it. I am very impressed that his manners trumped his feelings. I don't even know if I could have gone there, because I have a psychological aversion to the meat of animals I find especially adorable, like deer—the same goes for rabbit, lamb, and veal. My gag reflex kicks in. But I am very much a believer in not insulting a host, so perhaps I would have been able to choke down Bambi had it come to that.

Parsons used to have a lovely graduation at Riverside Church with a lunch afterward, to which we invited our honorary degree recipients. One year two of our guests were Sister Parish and Albert Hadley of Parish-Hadley, the legendary interior design firm. I was sitting at Mrs. Parish's table, and she was an incredible character. I said, "You must receive lots of awards and accolades," and she said, "No, this is the first since I was given a perfect-attendance medal as a young girl. It came with a pig."

Well, this award did not come with a pig. It came with a very odd lunch of sea scallops that I was pretty sure were raw. Sister Parish corroborated this when someone asked her, "How's lunch?"

"Terribly chic," she replied, "but inedible."

As much as I believe it's good manners to eat what's put in front of you as long as it won't send you into anaphylactic shock, I also believe that, when a host, you really need to think about what will suit your guests. I think it's bizarre when you assume no one is a vegetarian or has an allergy. It doesn't hurt to have a salad on the side so your vegan guests can fill up on that rather than having to struggle through the coq au vin.

This does seem to be a modern dilemma. I don't want to challenge the allergies, but they do seem to be proliferating at a frightening rate.

You see parents sometimes hovering over perfectly healthy and allergy-free children, saying, "Oh no, she can't! He can't!"

I think in those extreme situations children get to the point where they are afraid to disappoint their paranoid parents, and so they profess an aversion to pretty much everything but chicken nuggets, hold the sauce.

When I grew up, I don't remember anyone having allergies to food. I went all though elementary school and never knew anyone with any allergies at all. Certainly some allergies are deadly and all too serious, but if there's a way to make yourself a more flexible eater, I think you should.

I think it is good, though, that nonsmokers are protected

these days from the clouds of smoke that used to hover in every public space just a couple of decades ago. Can you believe there used to be a smoking section on airplanes? You could smoke in theaters. It hasn't been that long. I remember watching TV award shows and when they did a wide shot you'd see the lasers cutting through dense smoke that filled the auditorium.

I never took up smoking. When I was nine or ten, my father was diagnosed with pleurisy. It scared the daylights out of him, and he quit cold turkey. For years my mother would have one cigarette a day, in the evening. My grandmother smoked until the last day of her life. I still remember going to the doctor with her when she was in her eighties. Her doctor said she had to stop smoking.

"But it's one of the few things she still enjoys," I said. "Let her smoke!"

That's not to say I'm pro smoking. When I was at Parsons, I was sad that with each successive year, more students would smoke. Maybe it's declining now, but in that place at that time, it was definitely on the rise.

Not only did I not smoke, I didn't have a drink until I was thirty and moved to New York. Any association with alcohol was a turnoff because there was so much of it around my family.

Now, my mother denies this up and down, in spite of hard evidence. My grandmother had a huge box of correspondence. After her death, my mother and sister and I read these letters out loud, and I said, "Isn't it funny how often she talks about people drinking? Everyone was always drunk and falling off horses and wandering off into the woods." My mother insists they weren't drunks; they just knew how to have a good time.

Yes, I thought, *by getting loaded.*

Anyway, because of that association with booze, I would go out to people's houses and just have tonic water. Now, since moving to New York, I love having a drink now and then.

So maybe I'll grow to love sea slugs, too? I kind of doubt it.

When You Need Help, Get It

I'M CRAZY ABOUT MARTHA Stewart. We've done a lot of things together, and I've always loved watching her show. But sometimes her domesticity gets a little out of control.

One day I was watching her cooking show. While roasting a pan of nuts, she said something I have never forgotten: "Life has few disappointments greater than a room-temperature nut."

After Martha had been through the ordeal of her trial and jail time at what was referred to as Camp Cupcake, I asked her if she still stood by that quote.

"I said that?" she asked me.

"Yes," I said. "I think about it all the time."

"Well," she said, "I wouldn't say it now!"

FOR A 2009 SEGMENT for *The Dr. Oz Show,* I went to D.C. and met an extraordinary testimony to courage. My assignment was to help a veteran shop for clothes. Sgt. Reinita Gray is an amazing woman: a mother of five who did four tours of duty and lost her leg to a missile while on a noncombat mission in Iraq, earning her a Purple Heart.

She hadn't been out of the hospital since the loss of her leg, so we brought a special wheelchair van and I wheeled her in and out of it and through Bloomingdale's.

We had my usual fight about size.

"It's too small!" she insisted.

"It's not too small!" I said. "Look at the sleeves and the shoulders. It fits!"

We talked about all the outfits we thought were a hot mess. We teased each other. It was all such fun—and very moving. She's just learning to get around on her prosthetic leg, and one time she walked out of the Bloomingdale's dressing room unassisted.

But where it became even more inspiring was back at the hospital. The bigger picture of inspiration and emotion for me was being at Walter Reed Army Medical Center. While waiting in the lobby for our contact there, we saw people go by who were badly burned, completely bandaged. That was the visual. But when we went to the amputee center, the big wing at Walter Reed, we spent an hour or so in the physical therapy area, and would you believe I didn't see one person who looked miserable?

The spirit in that room was so uplifting. The room was full of people who had lost a limb or two or even more, and I expected to be met with individuals full of anger and self-pity and depressed by their situation, but instead they seemed so full of life. What they go through is incredibly tough. Sometimes it takes two years for these patients to build up the strength in their stumps so that the prosthetics will work. I felt almost joyous about the spirit of the human will. There was no self-pity in that room. The refrain was: I'm so happy still to be alive. Again and again, people said that to me, and they *smiled*.

That experience put so much in perspective for me. I tried to remember how many people seemed that happy and grateful the last time I was at a fashion event full of well-off, successful, gorgeously dressed guests eating wonderful canapés and drinking champagne. In high society, you have people walking around complaining that they haven't had their nails done in two weeks. Well, I want to say to them now, "At least you have nails to do! At least you have a hand!"

Maybe it's the gift of having become successful late in life, but I feel so incredibly lucky to have the life I do. I am blessed to work in a field I love, to do projects I care about, and to be appreciated for what I bring to the table. When someone hands me a glass of champagne, I sure don't check the label to see whether it's worthy of my consumption.

Back to Walter Reed. I thought these soldiers would be furious and sad. I spent a long time with Sergeant Gray, and we spoke very frankly, so I know she has moments of despair, but she pulls herself out of them. She is committed to moving forward. And that's a quality I saw in all of these soldiers: a total commitment to working hard and figuring out how to make the most of whatever they have.

"How do you rationalize this tragic accident to yourself?" I asked Reinita.

"I don't even try to," she said. "Things happen, and this happened. I'd like to think things happen for a reason. We never know why, but this has given me such a sense of who I am, independent of this leg I've lost. I've focused on my family in a way I hadn't before."

I have so much respect for her, and for everyone at that

hospital, and for all our veterans. Each day I think about them and the other people I've met in the course of my travels who are enthusiastic about their lives, and I try to remember them when I encounter someone who has everything—money, fame, and legs—and yet complains constantly about how hard they have it.

That's something the staff at Walter Reed has no patience for: whining. They give tough love. They are not coddling those patients with whom they spend so much time. When Reinita was struggling to get up from the mat on which she was doing her physical therapy, I bent down to get her crutches. The physical therapist shot me a look.

"I shouldn't do that?" I asked her.

She shook her head. And together we watched Reinita learn to stand up on her own.

I am so grateful to Dr. Oz for giving me the chance to go to Walter Reed, let alone to be a part of his core team. I always love appearing on his show, because I genuinely believe he's having a hugely positive impact on his viewers.

When the producers approached me about being a regular guest, I thought it might be fun. I had seen Dr. Oz on *Oprah* and liked his bedside manner. But it's been even more fulfilling than I anticipated. He has genuine warmth and a very clear and articulate way of communicating. He doesn't dumb things down, but the way he speaks is accessible (his producers have suggested that I with my fancy vocabulary don't always manage this . . .). He's not an alarmist, which is so refreshing.

I love the part of his show that teaches the audience about what is and isn't normal when it comes to their bodies. The audience has placards with NORMAL written on one side and

NOT NORMAL on the other, and they vote on topics before he explains the truth behind them. I learned that snoring was not normal, for example. There's a lot of content packed into his show. And I'm not surprised that he has one of the top daytime TV talk shows in America.

Dr. Oz was the one who wanted us to go to Walter Reed to take a look at the place and see what we could do, and it really did change my life. I am tempted to rent a bus and drive a bunch of self-involved New Yorkers down to D.C. to see the physical therapy wing. "We're going to take a little trip, people! Come with me, all you mopers!"

Can't you see Martha Stewart standing there in the middle of Walter Reed? She'd kill me for saying this, but I like to imagine the pre-Camp Cupcake Martha surveying the scene and then saying, "This is nothing compared to the disappointment of a room-temperature nut."

NOW I WANT TO talk seriously about people who aren't just depressed about their nails, but who are truly depressed or who are going through hard times without a staff of military doctors on hand. I have been there, and I want to reassure you that I know how impossible it feels. I promise you that things will get better if you are committed to climbing out of whatever hole you find yourself in.

First of all, there is no shame in undergoing therapy. I know there's still a stigma in much of the country, and I think that's too bad. Here in New York, the questions you hear most often are, "Where's your apartment?" and "Who's your therapist?"

I don't think everyone needs to go all the time (nor can everyone afford to), but I do think everyone at some point or other can benefit from a little chat with a psychologist, whether it's when the kids leave for college or when you've lost your job or when you've had a painful breakup or when someone close to you has died or when you've for no discernible reason lost the joy in life.

I think people are afraid to admit to problems, because once they admit to them, then those problems become real. But everybody has problems. If you think you don't have any, then you do have a problem. Being in denial or feeling you can't talk about things is so dangerous. You have to do *something* about whatever your struggles are. It's what gives us resources to move forward. It's what life *is*.

People get very defensive if they think you're saying what they're doing isn't normal. I don't think it's about normal. It's about acceptable. When we talk about a situation that we need to change, it's better not to think about whether or not it's normal, but instead about whether or not it's acceptable. Some things are contextual: People blow their noses on the street in India with no tissues. If you're over there, you can do that. But if you're on an American main street, you'd best break out the tissues.

Other things are never okay. It's not acceptable to be abusive to a family member, or for a child to behave destructively, or for a job to make you miserable. You need to figure out what to do about those things, and there's no shame in admitting you need a shrink, or your pastor, or your family, to help you out. It can make all the difference in the world just to have someone impartial to talk to once a week.

I say ever so glibly, "Go get some therapy," but the value depends on the quality of the therapist. There's a huge difference between a good one and a bad one. When I was young, my parents sent me to a lot of doctors, and some of them were far crazier than I was.

You have to shop around for someone who suits you. I think a therapist of the same gender sometimes helps with empathy, but you know when you've found someone you click with.

After trying a bunch of duds, eventually I wound up seeing a truly wonderful therapist five days a week—Dr. Phillip Goldblatt in New Haven, Connecticut. His sense of caring was palpable. He didn't have to say anything; I could just sense his goodness and concern. I had the maturity of a gnat and a lot of issues. He made me deal with them. It took a long time. He would keep returning to things that came up. He absolutely gave me my life back.

Why, you may be thinking, did I have to go to therapy five times a week? Well, it wasn't my idea, I'll tell you that. It was an intervention that was thrust upon me. I'll come clean: When I was seventeen, I made a serious suicide attempt. I was at yet another boarding school—I must have cycled through a dozen schools in as many semesters—and was ever more miserable. I had a debilitating stutter. I had no friends. I was incredibly lonely and depressed. I just wanted to end it all.

In my dorm room at Milford Academy I took far too many pills, then lay down to die with a sense of peaceful resignation.

Then, much to my frustration, I woke up the next morning. *This wasn't supposed to happen* was my first thought when I opened my eyes on a new day.

I hear that people who survive jumping off the Golden Gate Bridge report thinking on the way down that they want to live after all. When they survive, they feel so grateful. But I didn't have that feeling. I was disappointed that I'd failed.

Now, of course, I'm glad the pills didn't work.

I learned how to cope. I matured so much. When I got beyond my stutter at the age of nineteen, it reminded me of how I felt about the world when I was given glasses at the age of twelve. Everything changed. I hadn't known that you could see individual leaves on trees, or that you could read road signs from a car window. Similarly, when I could speak clearly, my world opened up. I could actually be comfortable talking to people. It was like being more fully whole. I realized I had been living only a partial existence.

Going through all that helped me be a better person and a better teacher. I feel so much compassion for what young people go through. It is very hard to grow up, especially when you're sensitive. You're so vulnerable at that age. I worry about my friends' children, and I try to be a good uncle.

The Megan Meier case, in which a teenager hanged herself after being tormented online by her friend's mother posing as a teenage boy, is an example of the worst kind of inhumanity. That case made me want to unplug the Internet.

Of course, you can't do that. You have to let young people live their lives. But you also have to do everything you can to show them that their teenage years are going to end and that there's a world of possibility out there. We all need to do anything we can do to help children realize that they have value and gifts to give the world.

Sometimes people ask me when I figured out that I was gay. Well, for a very long time, I didn't know *what* I was. I knew what I wasn't: I wasn't interested in boys, but I *really* wasn't interested in girls. A lot of it was denial, but it was also that I didn't feel unsatisfied. I've always loved working and have made that my priority. For many years, I described myself as asexual, and that's probably still closest to the truth.

I do believe in a spectrum of sexuality. Some people are completely straight and some are completely gay, and plenty of people are somewhere in between. I think it's crazy how hung up Americans, especially American men, are on this subject. I identify as gay, but there are women to whom I'm attracted. It's not like I want to go to bed with them—but I can appreciate when someone's radiating sexiness.

Things have changed so much in the past thirty years; it's almost hard for young people today to imagine what it was like to be gay back then. Let me tell you: It was the opposite of fun. You used to feel so alone with it all. If you were even thinking about homosexuality, you assumed it was only a matter of time before someone put you in a straitjacket. In my parents' home, the term wasn't even in our vocabulary. I used to think if I shared any of my thoughts, they would lock me up. If I tried to talk about anything even remotely related, my parents would say, "We've never heard of this!" But I think they knew that "this" was what I was, and that that's part of why they sent me to shrinks constantly.

To this day, my mother has never acknowledged that I'm gay. I'm *out* in public. I mean, I've been on the cover of *The Advocate*. But it wasn't until a couple of years ago that she finally stopped talking about women she wants to set me up with. When she met the man I was with for a decade, I introduced him as a dear friend I wanted her to meet. She didn't ask any questions then, and she never asked me what happened to him when he dropped off the face of the earth. I always half expect her to say, "Gay? I just thought you were *happy!*"

In fact, if there were ever a moment when my mother and I would have talked about my being gay, it would have been one night when we went out to dinner in the Village. It was the second and last time she visited me. In twenty-six years, she's been here only twice. I think my move to New York from Washington, D.C., was always hard for her. She found New York intimidating and always joked that she needed to lose a dress size and get a new wardrobe before she could visit.

I took her to Chez Ma Tante on West Tenth Street. We were sitting there waiting to order. She looked me right in the eyes and said, "Why would you take me to a restaurant where there are only men? Are they all *homosexual?*"

This stopped me cold.

"You don't know that everyone in here is gay," I said, trying to psych myself up for the conversation. "And furthermore, it's New York, in the Village, at the end of the twentieth century. For men to be together is normal and acceptable . . ."

There was a tense moment, and I thought I saw an awareness dawning on her. Then two women walked through the door, and my mother said, "Oh, never mind, there are some women!" And she went back to looking at the menu as if nothing were amiss. Denial is not just a river in Egypt.

Today's young people have Adam Lambert and Lady Gaga and the Internet, where they can find a support system.

That doesn't mean being a teenager (much less a gay teenager) is ever easy. The physical changes are enough to traumatize a person. I feel such sympathy for teenage boys who have that wisp of a mustache. They're too young to shave, but they're starting to look werewolf-y. If you're gay on top of it, it can be very scary if you live in a place that isn't supportive.

The Harvey Milk High School in New York City serves gay

teenagers who don't feel safe at other schools. When I moved from the West Village to the Upper West Side, I gave the school my grand piano, which had been a gift from my grandmother. I thought, *Those kids need it more than I do*. When you don't fit in, something like a piano, or a flair for design—whatever tools or talents you discover at that age—can show you a whole new world. One truly nice person or one thing that you learn to do well can save your life.

Back when I was a suicidal, seventeen-year-old, misfit boarding-school student, I never thought I would be where I am now. I never imagined that I'd have a beautiful apartment, or a job I loved, or witty friends. I think about that when fans on the street call out, "We love you, Tim!"

I want to respond, "I love you, too!" I mean it. I am so grateful for my wonderful fans' support. I hope in my honor they will think about the children in their lives who may be struggling and share that love with them.

Take Risks! Playing It Safe Is Never Really Safe

H OW I BECAME INVOLVED in *Project Runway* is a funny thing. The producers were looking for a consultant because they knew little about the fashion industry. They had produced *Project Greenlight,* about the film business, so this was a new world for them. A few people had given them my name, so they called me at Parsons.

I will tell you that I had my snob hat on as I was talking to them on the phone. *Fashion reality?* I thought. *That sounds disgusting. Who's telling them to call me—my enemies?*

I was reluctant to meet with them, but I agreed to go. Truth be told, I was a little curious. The meeting went very well. I was instantly more interested when they said they wanted to work with real fashion designers. I thought, *At least there's some integrity operating here.*

Then they asked me the question that, upon reflection, I realized they were using to vet people. "How would you feel if we told you we wanted the designers to design and create a wedding dress in two days?"

"Well," I said, very matter-of-factly, "they'd have to design and create a wedding dress in two days."

They looked at each other meaningfully.

"Did I give you the wrong answer?" I asked.

"No," they said. "You're just the first person who said it could be done."

"Why?" I asked. "What have you been hearing?"

"Everyone says it would take days, a minimum of a week, that they'd need help, that the process is so complicated . . ."

"Look," I said, "in two days you're not going to get an Oscar de la Renta wedding gown. You'll probably get a basic column without sleeves, but it will be a wedding dress."

They looked at each other again, and I thought I saw them smile.

I left the meeting feeling really excited about the project and hoping they'd pick me.

Then I waited and waited. I was feeling disappointed when they hadn't called a week later. But then a couple of days after that they did call, and they said they wanted to work with me. I was thrilled.

We worked together for six months, and there were just two major points of disagreement. During their fashion-industry interviews, they had become convinced that the designers shouldn't make their own clothes. In this scenario, there would be a sample room full of seamstresses and pattern drafters who would do the actual fabrication.

"Unless the audience sees the designers getting real and metaphorical blood on their hands, why would it care about them?" I asked. "Also, whom does Heidi send home? If there's any problem with the garment, the designer can just blame it on the seamstress."

We know I won that. The other point of disagreement had to do with the workroom. Originally, it was going to be in the Atlas apartments, where the designers would live. The belief was that they should have twenty-four-hour access to it. I said that would make the show a stamina test beyond the stamina test it already is. I insisted they be forced to go home at a specific time and then return the next morning.

Not only was it marginally better for them mentally and physically, it would give them some fresh perspective on their work, a break from what I call the monkey house.

I won that, too. (Essentially, the Bravo show *Launch My Line* is all the things I didn't want for *Project Runway*.)

In the end, they didn't have the budget to outfit Atlas with a loftlike workroom, so they were scrambling for an alternate space.

"Do you want to look at Parsons?" I asked.

Once the show was a success, people started speculating about how Parsons scored such a huge coup. Well, now it can be told!

I called downtown to Parsons headquarters and said we wanted the uptown design building for filming over the summer. I asked what the feeling would be and how, if it was indeed okay, we would facilitate it. The auditorium space where the judging happens had been used by outside people conducting seminars, and, ahem, sample sales. A staff person, Margo, was in charge of it. We talked to her about it, and *Project Runway* made a deal to pay the fee plus the cost of extra security and all the other expenses associated with keeping the building open after hours. Everyone was happy, or so I thought.

Two days before wrapping, one of the university's executive

VPs called and yelled at me. "I've just heard about this show!" she ranted. "You're putting this entire institution at risk!"

I didn't see the danger, but she kept insisting I had single-handedly destroyed the college.

"We're coming up and stopping this right now," she said.

I went to see Margo, who had received the same call I had. "What do we do?" she asked, starting to panic.

I thought about it for a second and then said, "I've been in academia long enough to know that when they say, 'We're on our way up there,' it will be a couple of days."

Sure enough, wrapping was long finished by the time the VPs arrived with their torches and pitchforks to shut it all down.

But I was still kicking around, so they took their anger out on me. I was royally raked across the coals by the Legal Department and by the president's office. They scolded and shamed and told me what a disgrace I was and how much jeopardy I'd put the college in. Finally, I asked, "What did I do wrong? I called and asked you about it. You said to work it out with Margo. We worked it out. You got a hefty chunk of change. What's the problem?"

Naturally, when the show was a big success, they were congratulating themselves on how bright they'd been to get in on the ground floor. I didn't remind them how they'd almost fired me over it. I just said, "You're right! Good job!" Take the high road.

The *Runway* producers were very hesitant to have me go on the auditions, because it was a lot of time and they weren't paying me, but I really wanted to go anyway. I was curious and wanted the show to succeed, and I said, "I've invested this much time and energy into this project. I'd like to stay involved through each phase and help get the right people for this."

So I followed them around to see the applicants. It was really interesting, and very hard work. We were doing twelve-hour days, looking through hundreds of portfolios and garments. In New York City, I did prescreenings out in the courtyard of the Soho Grand Hotel, where the interviews were being conducted, and I saw a procession of odd people who just wanted to be on a television show. They had brought clothing, but in some cases they were items from their closets, or pieces they had designed but not made. In some cases there were no clothes at all, just some drawings or photographs. It was a big potpourri.

I would say three-quarters were design students, and while I don't object to that in theory, they're still in an incubator. They almost never have their own point of view yet.

Some of the future stars of the show were in that line, and I had no early indication that they would make it on the show. Jay McCarroll, who went on to win Season 1, arrived pulling a wagon containing what I recall were dolls. Austin Scarlett was in the line looking incredibly androgynous and strange. Looking at the two of them, I thought: *Is this going to be a freak show?* But of course we wound up discovering some amazing talent, including Austin and Jay.

In Miami, on the last day of auditions, the producers came to my hotel room and said, "We think we need a mentor to be with the designers in the workroom. Would you be interested?"

I thought about it for a second and then asked, "Do I have to live with them?"

They laughed and said no, I wouldn't have to live with them.

"In that case, sure!" I said.

When I called my mother to tell her I was being considered for a TV show, she responded, "But you're so *old*."

"I think I'm meant to be a counterpoint to the young designers," I said. What I was thinking was, *Gee, thanks, Mom.*

But even then I still had to prove myself. Bravo needed what's called B-roll of me talking on TV. Luckily, I had done a couple of little fashion-related interviews that they could look at, including one on *CBS Sunday Morning*. Based on that, they gave me a chance. As you know by now, I've always been shy. *Project Runway* was either going to kill me or cure me. But I thought it was a great opportunity. I had to just do it and hope I didn't die from fright. It made it easier that I didn't think I was actually going to be on camera much, if at all.

No one has ever said this, but I am pretty sure that the producers speculated that if they just sent the designers alone into the workroom with a challenge, no one would talk. They would just work, heads down and eyes on their garments, and the tops of these designers' heads wouldn't make for must-see television. Sending me in to probe and ask questions would at least elicit some dialogue.

Accordingly, the entire time we were taping, I had every confidence no one would ever see me or hear my voice. I thought they were cutting me out and just leaving in the designers' responses. So I was very relaxed, assuming I was just a ghost on the cutting-room floor.

As we now know, they wound up leaving me in as a character. I was pretty shocked when I saw the first season and realized I was not a disembodied voice or a mere prompter. But I was happy with how smart the show was and how much it revealed about the creative process. The rest is history.

I was an unpaid consultant for the first two seasons, and then I signed with an agent and began being paid for my work, which made the situation even better.

People are often shocked to hear that I was unpaid for so long, but I did it for the love of it, and (please don't read this, anyone associated with the show) I would do it again for free in a heartbeat. And it all worked out. My West Village apartment was falling apart, so even though I couldn't afford it at the time, I joined a waiting list for a more expensive place called London Terrace Gardens on West Twenty-third Street. I was nervous that my name was going to come up before I could afford it, but luckily, it wasn't until I was given the appointment at Liz Claiborne Inc. that my name was called, and by then I had the means to move.

Yes, those early days of *Project Runway* were hard work, but they were also deeply fulfilling. What if I'd said no because I wasn't being paid? I would have turned my back on an incredible opportunity. I wanted to help them because I was concerned with the quality of the show. I wanted it to show reverence for this industry I love and prevent anyone from making a joke out of it. Luckily, the producers were all about quality and integrity. It was a great marriage.

What do they say: Do what you love and the money will follow? It's always been true for me. I had no expectation of personal success through this show. I never expected there would be a second season, much less a seventh. And I never expected to get famous in a million zillion years. While we were making Season 1, I just thought, *If nothing else, this is going to be great cocktail-party-conversation fodder.*

Lauren Zalaznick arrived during the taping of one of the Season 1 shows. I didn't know she was the president of Bravo and so, technically, our boss. We were just two people stand-ing there together in the back of the auditorium watching the judging together. She turned to me and asked rhetorically, "Who's going to want to watch this?"

"You're corroborating my worst fears," I responded. It was hard back then to see the shape of the show. I didn't know what was going on when I wasn't around. I thought, *Is it going to be about sexual escapades at the Atlas?*

But now we know how it turned out: a smart, fun look in-side the creative process of fashion designers. I was so happy about it. It proved the point I keep insisting on: You don't need to dumb things down for the television audience. People are smart, and they want to see intelligent shows. People have come up to me and said *Project Runway* is the thinking man's reality show, an idea I love. The audience for the premiere of Season 1 was 354,000. For Season 6, it was almost three mil-lion.

It was very satisfying to come back to some of the snarkier people in the industry—the ones who said way back during the airing of Season 1 that I was wasting my time or that the show wouldn't amount to anything—and to tell them, "Remember that show you were so dismissive of? It was just nominated for an Emmy."

To date, the show's been nominated for sixteen Emmys. There's a bobble-head doll of me for sale. I am well known enough that there is a ton of misinformation floating around about me on the Internet. There was something about my going to the deli across the street from my office with Andy Roddick. They said we were dating and had a lover's spat at the counter. Well, I've never even met Andy Roddick but he's married to a woman, and I haven't been on a date in decades, so no chance of that! But I'm flattered that people think of me enough to take the time to make up insane gossip.

Again, no one's more shocked or pleased than I am at how the show took off and changed so many lives. I guess it really did seem like a dubious undertaking back then. We had scores of potential judges turn us down. I called Diane von Fürstenberg at least twice to ask her to judge, and she turned me down.

"I told you," she said in that catlike voice of hers, "I'm not interested in doing this show. I'm going to my island."

When the show premiered, she called and said, "Why didn't you tell me about this? It's wonderful!"

(Quick anecdote: Diane von Fürstenberg's 2009 Christmas card featured a foldout poster of her as the mermaid figurehead of a ship. Well, it turns out that image was not a product of Photoshop. It was the actual bow of the yacht belonging to her husband, Barry Diller. I hadn't seen anything like that since Michael Jackson's *History* video.)

Heidi Klum is a key creative force behind *Project Runway*. I love her. She's just utterly and totally fantastic and has believed in the idea from the start. But that's not to say all the negative talk about the show couldn't get to her, too. To add to the anxiety of Season 1, we were doing pickup lines as filler. We don't do that anymore, but back then we had to do that occasionally when the plot was too confusing. So we're sitting in a hotel suite, waiting to do our lines, and she looks genuinely devastated. I said to her, "Heidi, you look really upset. Is anything wrong?"

"Have you seen an advance cut of the show?" she asked me.

"No, why?" I said. "Have you?"

"Yes, I think it's great. But a friend who saw it said it was bad, and now I'm worried." She was especially upset because this was someone in the TV world.

"You can't listen to anyone in TV!" I told her. "Everyone in this business has an agenda. We're not going to know if it works until the public sees it."

That seemed to calm her down, but I wasn't surprised she was so upset. Heidi doesn't respond well to criticism. Someone who's that beautiful certainly doesn't face a lot of it in the course of her life!

And yet, secretly, I was wondering, *Is the show terrible?*

As we all know now, Heidi never should have worried. And I was right to believe in her and the show and to risk getting on board. I also learned that working on something you believe in and that you enjoy is really no risk at all.

There are attendant risks to fame, though, like going to awards shows. The first time I walked the red carpet, I felt like a mongrel at the Westminster Dog Show. When we were nominated for our first Emmy for Season 1 of *Runway*, I was beside myself. The entrance had bleachers that were packed with photographers flanking the carpet.

People kept yelling at me things like, "You're blocking my view of Jessica Walter!"

It was humiliating. At the end of the row were curtains, and when I reached them, I thought I was finally going to be inside and away from all the flashbulbs and shouting. But no: It was just beginning.

The NBC publicist wouldn't let me hide. She kept saying to the press, "I have Tim Gunn here. Do you want to talk to him?"

Looking right at me, they would say, "Who?"

Then we lost on top of it!

I have such respect for people who do the red carpet, because it's so hard. Everyone wants to criticize what you're wearing. Every news channel wants to have the most captivating story to tell, so they're dying to have someone trip or to see the top of a strapless dress fall off.

This is a circumstance where taking a fashion risk is an incredibly brave and hard thing to do, and I celebrate it.

Whenever I do red-carpet reportage, celebrities come up to me because they know I will ask real questions and won't cheer if they fall down. Once on the red carpet, the goddess Helen Mirren reached over and gave me a big kiss and said, "That's for saying such nice things about me at the Oscars."

But I wasn't just being nice. I can't lie, so I am incapable of being a kiss-up. I really thought she was the most ravishing, sexy woman there. She is absolutely amazing because she is so comfortable in her skin. She exudes that. And she wasn't afraid to show it off.

And yet, I've received plenty of flak for things I've said as a commentator.

Once was when I stood in support of the black lace Alexander McQueen dress Cate Blanchett wore to the 2007 Golden Globes. It was kind of a minidress with a big black lace skirt and train over it. I thought it was great. I asked her about it, and she said, "I only listen to my own voice. I'm surrounded by people who want to make me into their dress-up doll. But this was a collaboration between Alexander McQueen and me, and it's exactly what I wanted."

I loved it, and so did *People,* but we were about the only ones. The press went to town on me for approving of it and basically said I'd lost my mind. Well, I don't think so. I stand by that dress.

Something similar happened at the 2008 Oscars when Tilda Swinton wore a washed silk satin black Lanvin gown. I thought she was magnificent. I had a debate with Stacy London on *Today* about it. She said it was a big garbage bag. But I insisted the dress said exactly what Tilda wanted it to. That Lanvin creation said, "I am not a classicist. I am a bohemian. I stand apart. My clothes say that about me."

Would I put that dress on Sally Field? Of course not. You can't separate the dress from the woman who's wearing it. That's the point I try to make when I talk about "the semiotics of fashion"—that is, what our clothes say about us.

There's only one judgment I regret. After the 2009 Oscars, I was on *Good Morning America* and debating someone with whom I've never particularly gotten along. She made me so crazy that I became a contrarian. I am usually very polite and measured, but when someone gets my hackles up, I tend to blurt out ridiculous things just to disagree. And, alas, this occasionally happens on national television.

This morning-show nemesis of mine said something about Sophia Loren's organza Armani gown. You may remember the dress. It was low-cut, full of pleats and ruffles, and wouldn't have been out of place on a Wild West madam. Suddenly, I became the dress's sole, and impassioned, defender. "She didn't look inappropriate," I said righteously. "She didn't look like a tart!"

But you know what? She totally did.

I met her and Valentino on the same red carpet, and I thought, *They would make a great match, just in terms of their completely unnatural coloring, a similar otherworldly shade of orange-bronze.*

RISK TAKING IN FASHION is fun, but risk taking in our careers and in our education is essential. Ambitious people are more attractive and more fun to be with than people who maintain the status quo.

I love it when at least one designer on *Runway* is eager to step up and out. Typically, the whole cast is ambitious, but sometimes only one or two of them have that intense drive to take it to the next level. They want to make a positive mark on the world. They want to leave a legacy.

I lived in Kuala Lumpur, Malaysia, for four months when we were establishing a Parsons program there in partnership with the Malaysian government. The prime minister's daughter had gone to Parsons in New York. He loved the education she received so much that he asked us to set something up there. There are few design schools in Malaysia, and I found out why.

In a group of potential faculty, I was talking about a competitive environment in the classroom and how this is a good thing. I said the faculty has to have a high bar of expectation, and the students themselves need to push one another. They stared at me like I was crazy. I was clearly speaking a foreign language. What was revealed was that in that part of the world, it's not good to be better.

I hear this is also a Midwest sensibility, and that in certain states bragging is forbidden. I'm stunned by it. No one can be better than the lowest common denominator?

I remember from my admissions days the demise of class ranks on high school transcripts. They stopped probably twenty years ago. For me, sitting in an admissions seat, ranks were a way of assessing the 3.6 from a high school. Is that in the top 10 percent, or does everyone else at that school have a 4.0? When I asked high school officials why they'd gotten rid of ranks, I was told, "Ranks made students feel bad."

Well, if they're in the bottom 5 percent of their graduating class, maybe they should feel bad!

I thought it was a woeful day when they took ranks away. Everyone needs a push to reach what he's capable of.

This was my point in Malaysia: You need to differentiate between good, mediocre, and poor. In my Western experience, we want to achieve our best. We want the gold star. The golden apple! To think that all I have to do is show up and I'll be patted on the head? That's no way to live an exciting artistic life.

I SEE THIS AS a trend not just in academia but also in parenting. I think it may be the celebration of imagination and self-confidence over good citizenship. Creativity should be fostered, but so should conceptual development and execution. Parents should want their children's self-confidence to be earned.

I love to see children building discipline, whether it's by learning an instrument or doing a sport. It's good to expose them to lots of different things. A broad range of exposure is really important, because you don't know what's going to resonate. But when you find something that does it for them—

whether it's the ballet or baseball or sewing or karate—you can feel good that you helped them find something they can get involved in and about which they feel motivated to excel.

We adults need to do this, too. It takes a certain level of humility to push ourselves to try new things. Once we have a realm of expertise, we may think, *Why expand our horizons? We've found our niche.* But it's very important to keep your hand in as broad a range of areas as possible. I've seen so many people around me losing their jobs in recent years, and some have had a very tough time readjusting.

My advice to them: Try to take your ego out of it. You don't make it about you and how hard your life is. You have to focus on what needs to get done and find a way to do it, independent of what your ego may be saying about what you deserve or what's beneath you.

I ran into a neighbor at the supermarket who had lost his job on Wall Street. He was there at the store applying for a job. He showed me the application and said he'd just had an interview and they'd told him he was overqualified. "But I'll do anything," he pleaded. He was having a hard time, but he had the right attitude, and I predicted he would come out of the recession just fine.

Breadth of exposure is really important in education, even if you're studying something specific like fashion. At Parsons we made our students experience every phase of every design. They would bitterly complain: "I don't want to do menswear," or "I can't do children's clothes." But they would have epiphanies. "Wow, I'm really good at suits." Or "I have a natural gift for children's pajamas."

They would be amazed, and I would say, "That's why we do this." They never would have discovered it otherwise. They would have cut themselves off from a rich field of experience if they'd had their choice.

The buffet style of education, where you take what you want when you want it, is so unfortunate, in my opinion. I know young people. They gravitate toward what comes naturally to them and what they think they want. But what they're comfortable with isn't necessarily their destiny.

I also think it's good to keep as wide a circle as possible of professional acquaintances. My predecessor at Parsons never interviewed anyone for positions unless there was one available that very second. I took a lot of promising people out for lunch just so we'd know each other and be able to cut to the chase when a job did open up. I thought we should vet people and stay in touch with them so we had a stable and could get someone into open jobs immediately rather than having everything be a 911 call.

You can be inspired by anything, and you never know what information is going to serve you well later. That's why I think core curriculums are good. You need to have a grounding in everything. Fashion does not exist in a cultural vacuum. Lady Gaga's famous gyroscope dress on *Saturday Night Live* made me think that her designer at some point took a physics class.

So it's good to push yourself and others to study as many different fields as you can, even if you think you know exactly what you want to do.

If you aren't convinced that it's good for you and for your career, then maybe you will be convinced by David Sedaris's argument for broad-based education in his story "21 Down": "When asked 'What do we need to learn this for?' any high school teacher can answer that, regardless of the subject, the knowledge will come in handy once the student hits middle age and starts working crossword puzzles in order to stave off the terrible loneliness."

As a crossword puzzle junkie myself, I love that argument for education. But I also believe culture can genuinely improve your life. You can be too rich and too thin, but you can never be too well read or too curious about the world.

Give Back (but Know Your Limits)

M Y MOTHER PARTICIPATES IN one of those sponsor-a-child programs and has a boy in Guatemala to whom she sends money each month. She's been doing it for a long time.

"He sent me a Christmas card," she said that first holiday season.

"That's so sweet," my sister said. "What's his name?"

"Felix."

"Felix?" we said. "That doesn't sound very Guatemalan. What's his last name?"

"Wait," my mother said. "Let me get the card . . . It's Navi-dad."

She thought the name of her sponsored child was "Merry Christmas."

We still joke about Mr. Felix Navidad.

I am a firm believer in giving back, and I encourage you to do as much charity work as you possibly can—especially if your work allows me finally to take a break. In fact, in writing this book, I've been surprised by how often I've said things that could fall under the theme It's Hard to Be Nice.

That's not saying you shouldn't be nice for society's sake, nor that it doesn't ultimately pay off for you personally, but let's be honest: Niceness can at times feel a little bit thankless.

My wonderful associate, Marsha, and I have lunch together in my office every day when we're both free. At one recent lunch she was teasing me about how many charity lunches I go to. We took a bet on how many it actually was, and then we got out the calendar. A little math later, we realized I had attended more than sixty such lunches in the past year. That's more than one a week, far more than I see my family or my closest friends.

It's a hard thing to complain about. And no one knows this more than I do, having spent most of my life far from the in crowd. But please indulge me. There is this expectation that once you're in a certain social world, you have endless obligations to it.

I was at a reception for Bill Clinton at someone's apartment on Park Avenue, and as thrilled as I was to be there on one level, on another, I was just so drained from a long day of work that my idea of a good time involved getting under the covers with a book. While I was there, I was thinking how ironic it was that at one time I would have killed to be at this party. Now I would kill to be home watching game shows.

But maybe part of the problem is that I am just too clueless to move in high society. I'm often struck by how unworldly I am. A lot of invitations I get are receptions or dinners where you're expected to write a check, especially if it's for a political figure or a cause. And there I am showing up, ready just to have a drink and gossip, when in fact I'm supposed to be calculating how many thousands of dollars I have to hand over. I've realized I need to read the fine print.

The worst part is that the hosts are always surprised when I'm surprised. "Why did you think we were having this party?" they say when I stumble at the check-writing portion of the evening.

"Um, for fun?" I am so naïve.

IT FEELS RIDICULOUS TO complain about a call from Bette Midler, but I feel like I can, because it's not like she ever calls just to chat. It's always about an event. Not long ago, she called to invite me to a fund-raiser for the New York Restoration Project, her tree-planting initiative here in New York City. Well, it wasn't really an invite as much as an order. "You are coming to this event I've having, aren't you?" she said. "And you are buying a tree, aren't you?"

I did go, and I bought two trees, and it was all perfectly charming—but also, like all these things, a little painful. I was sitting next to Martha Stewart at the dinner, and the second Bette stood up to speak, Martha vanished. I turned around and she was just gone, without a trace.

"Where did she go?" I whispered to someone at the table.

"When she knows she's about to get hit up for money, she does a disappearing act," the person replied.

I should have her teach me that trick, I thought.

It's harder on people who, unlike me, have really serious money. My friend Dr. Sheila C. Johnson, who founded and ran Black Entertainment Television with her now ex-husband, received 1.5 billion dollars in a divorce settlement. We go to events together occasionally, and I'm always struck by how shameless people are in asking her for money wherever she goes. Her mother's friends are forever calling her, asking for $7 million for the church or some such thing, and she's always telling her mom, "Please stop telling your friends I will give them money. It's my money, and I will choose what to do with it!"

For the last event we went to together, I suggested we make a train of gold foil coins to attach to her gown. It would trail behind her to announce, "The horn of plenty has arrived!"

IN CASE YOU HAVEN'T guessed by now, I'm at these kinds of events all the time. I can't get more than a sip of a glass of wine at a party because I'm getting pulled this way and that for press or for work or for the show. There's no air in my schedule.

I know it's a high-class problem, and I'm the luckiest guy in the world. After being a poverty-stricken academic for so long, I am glad I can now afford to write checks occasionally to benefit worthy causes. But now that I'm not broke I have problems a lot more complicated than deciding which flavor of ramen noodles to cook up. Specifically: When do all the pleas for money stop? When I run out of cash and am back to the ramen?

This is one of the pitfalls of being nice: You wind up overextending yourself. That's why one of the most important things to learn after you master good behavior is how to say no gracefully. It's ultimately better for everyone, because you don't burn out and wind up in a mental institution, making you no good to anyone at all.

Slowly but surely, I'm learning where to draw the line and what does or doesn't make sense when it comes to do-gooding and to time commitments.

I ran the Parsons Fashion Benefit for years. I enjoyed doing it, but it kept getting more and more overwhelming, and I started to realize people would have gladly paid more not to attend. I constantly sat in opposition to what the party planners thought was best for the event. My belief is: Shorter is better. Always. But the people in charge always thought the more money people were spending the longer the evening should be. Wrong! They want to go home.

We have to rethink these things. It should be about collecting the money and saying thanks. A French luxury-goods organization used to have a ridiculously lavish benefit every year. *How much did the food cost?* I always wondered. *The flowers? How much money is left after all this?*

I DO A LOT of speaking engagements and love it. In spite of how formal I look with my suits and ties, I try to keep lectures very casual and relaxed. I don't like podiums. I like to walk around. And I keep track of how the audience is responding. If they seem bored, I just stop altogether. I usually designate someone in the front row to keep track of the time for me and to raise her arm when it's time to wrap it up.

At that point, we can have a Q&A, or we can just leave. Teaching helps me to do a decent job with pretty much any auditorium full of students, because I can really read a room. I'm lucky to have this skill and the humility to put it into practice. By contrast, celebrities typically come with a script and don't know how to improvise or wrap up quickly if things go off track.

The worst ever was Phil Donahue. He was an honoree at a benefit, and I was presenting an award after his acceptance speech. I heard the stage manager remind him that he had three minutes to speak, but he talked for forty minutes. Forty minutes. It was mind-numbing. The first thing I said when I walked out was, "I've completely forgotten what I was going to say." It got a big laugh.

Recently I was at a college event. There was to be a talk, then a Q&A, and then a forty-five-minute book signing. The schedule was mapped out, and I was looking forward to getting back to the hotel by nine thirty p.m. even if it ran over. I could almost taste the room service.

During the Q&A, I noticed that a third of the audience had left, and I thought, *I really must have droned on.* But no, they were all in line for the book signing, a signing planned for no more than fifty people. Several hundred were already lined up. When I realized this, I thought, *Uh-oh.* There was no one to save me, and I didn't want to disappoint anyone, so I just bit the bullet and kept signing. I was there until one a.m. and was a wreck the next day.

I am trying to get better at saying no. Someone gave me these hilarious cards to hand out that, instead of a name and phone number, simply say, "Thanks, but no thanks." I'm too polite to use them, but they crack me up.

Once at a book signing, a woman came back to the table, pointed at her signed book, and said accusatorily, "You didn't sign this!"

I looked at the book.

"Yes, I did," I said. "Right there."

"You printed!" she said angrily. "That's what I expect from an elementary school student! I want a signature."

I explained to her that that *is* my signature. That's how I sign a check. I print, because I studied architecture at one point and block printing rather than cursive became ingrained in me.

She ranted and raved to anyone who would listen about how I didn't sign her book. Luckily, there are a thousand lovely people for every one like that.

But let's talk some more about the bad ones, because they're the most fun to gossip about, and they deserve a little public shaming.

I receive a lot of fantastic e-mails from fans. I don't have time to respond to all of them, though I read them all. I feel so lucky that so many lovely people enjoy what I do. Only, some love me a little too much! One woman in Chicago said that her boyfriend said he'd marry her if I performed the ceremony.

I wrote her back. I said I'm not ordained, and I'm not a ship's captain or we could go out on Lake Michigan, so she should tell her boyfriend it's not going to happen. I wrote that if they loved each other, they should go ahead and get married.

She thanked me but made another appeal. "Tell me when you'd be available," she replied, quite seriously.

At that point, I'd already gone out of my way. Her expectations were way too high. And I think that's a good lesson for all of us. Don't try to manipulate other people into responding. Remember Rule 2: The World Owes You . . . Nothing? Well, I want to tell these people, I also owe you nothing! I mean, I am happy to pose for pictures, sign autographs, and participate in shows and speaking engagements that people might find entertaining or useful, but once I do all that, I don't have a lot to give.

A father has been stalking me since my Parsons days about meeting with his daughter and giving her an indoctrination into the fashion industry. They showed up at a book signing in New Jersey and cornered me. I was, I thought, lovely to them both. I talked to his daughter and encouraged her to go to a summer program when she's sixteen (she was eleven at the time). *That's done,* I thought, when I'd exhausted my advice and moved on to the next person on line.

But no. Still the father calls me every three months to plead for a Liz Claiborne Inc. tour for this daughter, a girl whom I can't imagine is as desperate to see our conference room as her father thinks she is. It really does seem to be all about him and what he wants for her rather than what she wants for herself.

If she is in fact just as pushy, then she has my pity. In my world, the squeaky wheel doesn't get the grease. Instead, I just stack the sandbags higher. People have even called my boss and said I wasn't being responsive!

Well, I immediately shut out anyone who does something tacky like that. I will write to the person and say, "I must not have been making myself clear. This isn't going to happen." It's like negotiating with terrorists. You can't let rude people win.

Hilariously enough, it's frequently the people who hold themselves up as paradigms who are the worst behaved. The countess from *The Real Housewives of New York City* wrote an etiquette book and e-mailed to tell me she'd told her publisher that I might write the foreword. I thanked her for asking me, but said I had a conflict of interest with my own publisher and so would have to decline.

She responded that if I wouldn't do it, she'd write it for me.

I said, "Ha-ha. Very funny."

"I'm serious," she said. This was for a manners book!

Perhaps sometimes forewords are really written by the author and then reviewed and signed by the foreworder and this was what she was contemplating, but I'd already made it clear that the issue wasn't about having time to write but with using my name.

I told her that if she was serious, then her lawyer should talk to my lawyer.

I never heard more from her.

IF YOU DON'T SET boundaries, it can get to the point where nothing's ever enough.

Case in point: I joined the board of directors of GMHC, the wonderful AIDS organization that I've long supported. I've hosted the event Fashion Forward for them since its inception and have been happy to do so. But then they made me a board member, about which I felt thrilled and honored at the time. I didn't think it would change my life very much, but it totally did. Suddenly, I was signing letters asking people for money. And I kept hearing back from fancy people saying, "If I help you with GMHC, you need to help me with this." I really couldn't give any more time or money to anyone, so I thought, *I need to scale back here.*

After much consideration, I said I had to bow out as a board member.

Well, guess what? They wouldn't let me. Their CEO said, "'No' to me means 'later.' You can just do these things for us later."

She said using my name had really helped them, and that was enough.

"Really?" I asked.

"Really," she said and talked me down off the ledge.

She reassured me that I was off the hook and they would stop asking me to do things all the time.

I relaxed and thought, *Phew, no more obligations, no more invites, no more events.* Two hours later I got an e-mail from her asking when I could go on a retreat!

Luckily, I now have an agent who handles charity requests, and he can say no for me. What I've learned from him is that boundaries are very liberating. They can be readjusted all the time, but it's important to have them. Always. When you don't have a shopping list, you can easily go astray in the cereal aisle. If you burn out, no one's going to benefit. So it's in everyone's interest for you to do what you can and then make it clear that you can do no more.

Carry On!

NOW THAT WE'RE WRAPPING up our conversation, I think it's time to talk about the eternal mysteries. I was raised as a loose Episcopalian, but I'm fascinated by all religions. God knows they're at the core of every society and culture on this planet. I'm also fascinated by the ceremony of it. But I haven't been to a church since my niece was baptized, and she's now twenty-three. None of the weddings I've been to since then have been in a church. I consider myself an agnostic, because I believe there are many things we don't fully comprehend.

Going to church was not my favorite thing when I was young. From a very early age, I was very suspicious of our priest. My parents thought I was crazy and just trying to get out of going to services, but I said, "No, there really is something weird about that man."

Indeed, one day when I was nine or ten, the priest was up at the pulpit. He went into a silent prayer and . . . never came out of it. After a few minutes the ushers realized he'd left the plane of reality the rest of us were on, so they had an intervention and took him away.

And yes: I smiled very smugly at my parents all the way home.

That's the mind-set I had when I went to see a psychic once about thirty years ago. I was in the middle of a personal and professional crisis. A dear friend, who is a clinical psychologist said she'd been to see this psychic, had an amazing experience, and encouraged me to go, too.

I scoffed and said, "One of those people with a neon sign?"

"No," she said, "I did my homework. This woman Jean MacArthur works three months of the year each in New York, Paris, London, and Washington. She's a consultant to NASA and the FBI."

Why not? I thought. I'm certainly not a crystal person or an astrology person, but I figured it would be good for a laugh if nothing else. I went with another friend of Pat's named Molly. Molly is a dear friend of mine, too; she's the painter with whom I shared a studio during my years as a sculptor. She's extremely smart and doesn't suffer fools gladly, so for her also to agree to see this person was disarming to me.

I was so disappointed when Jean MacArthur answered the door, because I was expecting to see Isadora Duncan, and instead she looked like the checkout lady at the Safeway. She looked very haggard and had scars running along her neck. She shook my hand, and we sat down. She told me to write down my date of birth. Then she said that I couldn't lie to her, and that whatever I said to her went through God and back to her and vice versa.

I was sitting there thinking, *This is ridiculous.*

"You will put your work as an artist on the shelf," she told me. "This will happen soon. You will enter the academic arena."

I was thinking, *Fat chance.* I hated school.

She told me a lot of things about my father that I thought she couldn't have known without talking to him or other members of my family. *Did she talk to Molly in advance?* I wondered.

She said she didn't believe in talking about prior lives because such talk wasn't useful, but then she paused and said, "However, I have never met a new soul . . . until today."

I can still hear her saying that, and it still gives me chills. It's not that I put any factual stock in it, but there was something about it that sounded right somehow. When she said that, I thought, *New soul is at least an apt metaphor for my openness and sometimes naïve belief in people.* I'd just had my heart broken, and felt duped and humiliated, and I liked that notion of "new soul" more than "fool."

"Whatever I see in my third eye I will never share unless it's something you can change," she said next. "If I tell you the train's coming, watch out—that means you have a shot at getting out of the way. But if the train's going to hit you no matter what, why say anything?"

I thought that was kind of a relief, and kind of a disappointment. After our session, she told me about all these surgeries she'd had. She said her third eye takes a terrible physical toll on her. I left my session thinking, *What a charlatan.*

Meanwhile, when Molly left her appointment, she looked stricken and said, "I have to see a doctor. Jean said something's wrong with my blood."

Molly went to an appointment with her doctor. There was nothing wrong with her. The doctor said, "What sent you to me?" and she was too embarrassed to say. So Molly and I said many disparaging things about Jean MacArthur.

The next week, Molly's identical twin sister was diagnosed with aplastic anemia, a form of leukemia. Again, I don't believe in psychic phenomena, but we found that quite spooky at the time.

And even if I am not a believer, I did find that meeting incredibly useful. I still think about Jean's train-wreck analogy whenever I talk to the *Project Runway* designers. I talk to them only about things they can change.

If we get back from Mood and they've bought only red fabric, I don't say, "Gee, it's too bad you didn't get green!"

It doesn't advance the plot. That's why I wasn't that thrilled by Nina's words to the designers the day before the Bryant Park show in the Season 6 finale: "If you have anything referential, get rid of it!"

Get rid of it? The show was the next morning—a little late for replacing a whole look. Nina tends to talk about things the designers can't change. Editors go there more than teachers. Editors are all about changing and improving all the time— which is what makes them so great and valuable to the industry, but it also makes them a little infuriating when there are unavoidable constraints. I like to talk only about the way things are, not the way they would be in an ideal world.

Maybe that's why I like etiquette so much: manners help us deal with the way things are, with the place we find ourselves in, whatever that is. Rules of behavior come in handy when you can't think straight, as when you're extremely happy or sad over a major event like a birth or a death.

Funerals are especially tricky for people. At your most emotional you suddenly have to do some very complex logistics, usually involving last-minute travel reservations, car rentals, and ironing.

Which reminds me—one tip for the men out there: Make sure you have a nice dark suit and tie. Even if you never have cause to wear them in the rest of your life, you will need one for funerals. It's shocking how many men in their thirties don't own a tie and don't even know how to tie one! Even if you don't need one for weddings, you need one for funerals. What message are you sending if you show up in a sweatsuit to a funeral? It's a basic lack of respect. Every man needs a suit. Okay, end of lecture.

I should tell you about my father's funeral in the mid-nineties. He's been dead for more than fifteen years, and before that he'd been in a nursing home with Alzheimer's for seven years. And yet, between you and me, I'm still not completely over his death.

When I went home years ago for the Thanksgiving holidays, my father was in the hospital with a bleeding ulcer. My mother and I went to see him, and he was pulling his IVs out and very disoriented. They had to restrain him. That's how bad it was.

Well, the next morning, Thanksgiving Day, his doctor asked us into his office, and he had a social worker in the room with us. I thought, *What are all these people doing here on Thanksgiving? This must be serious.* Sure enough, the doctor said that my father had Alzheimer's and told my mother, "This will ruin you financially. This will tear your entire family apart. And your husband will lose his soul."

In other words: *Happy Thanksgiving!*

When we left, we were both shaken up, but in the parking lot Mother turned to me and said, angrily, "What does that doctor know about our financial circumstances? Or the strength of our family? This won't tear us apart. And that's ridiculous that your father will *lose his soul*. How overdramatic."

When we got home, the phone was ringing. My father was restrained, but he had access to a phone and he kept calling over and over again, every minute and a half. Mother got to the point where she wouldn't answer it. My niece was a year and a half or so, and she kept pointing to the phone every time it rang, saying, "Pop! Pop! Pop!" which was her name for him. She knew it was Pop calling. It was very cute, and very depressing. Finally, we took the receiver off the hook.

The first time we went to visit Dad at the nursing home, we brought Raffles, our family's beloved dog and a favorite of my father's. She pulled out of her leash and collar, ran through the place straight to my father, and jumped in his arms. She'd never been there before, but she knew exactly where to find her master. Every time from then on, we'd let Raffles loose at the front door, and she'd run to my father and jump onto his lap, tail wagging.

Cut to year six in the nursing home. We brought Raffles, and that time she didn't bolt down the hallway. She didn't even want to go into Dad's room. She treated this man she used to worship like he was a foreign piece of furniture. At this point he really was a vegetable. I looked at my sister and said, "That doctor was right. His soul is gone."

It was another full year before he actually died, of a congestive lung problem, but for that year, as much time as we spent with him, he was a stranger to us and we to him.

We were offered an autopsy to conclusively determine that it was Alzheimer's. My mother asked my sister and me what we wanted to do, because there was concern about the disease being genetic. I had mixed feelings about it, so I asked my mother what she wanted to do. She said she thought maybe she would rather he didn't go through any more indignities, so we decided to forgo the autopsy.

Besides, we were pretty sure of what it was. My father was fairly young when he died: sixty-seven. His mother had died in a mental hospital at age sixty-seven, too. That was in the early 1950s. I'm thinking that she must have had the same disease, and they didn't know what to do with her, so they assumed she was crazy.

By the time my father was the age I am now, he'd already been diagnosed. Knock wood, I'm okay. And I'm ever vigilant about my mental health. I'm the first person waving down a flight attendant to tell her that the magazine's crossword has been filled in and to request a new one. Puzzles keep your brain sharp; at least that's what I'm counting on.

My mother still has her wits very much about her, and I think I'm a lot more like her than I am like my father. That said—if I start counting quarters and handing them to you to recount, you'll know it's too late. My father kept change in pill bottles. He would fill up a pill bottle, then pour out the coins count them, put them back in, and hand it to me to count. You can't ask why. When someone is past the threshold of Alzheimer's, you treat them the way you would an infant or very young child.

Now to the funeral: I am all in favor of cremation, but my father had never specified what he wanted, so we did the traditional thing. For some reason lost to time, we were having him buried in Ebensburg, Pennsylvania. Although Dad grew up in Cleveland, I believe his mother was from Pennsylvania.

My sister and her family were on the other side of Pennsylvania, so my mother and I stopped there overnight on the way to the funeral.

As we're driving on through Pennsylvania the next day, it's cold and starting to snow. We're all off in our own worlds. I'm staring out the car window at the winter weather, and suddenly, I have this flash: I left the garment bag with my suit at my sister's, on the other side of the state. The wake was that very evening. The funeral was early the next morning. It was small-town America. It was Sunday. No shops were open. I had on a pair of casual khakis.

I started laughing hysterically. When I announced my dilemma, Wallace, my niece, who was then about seven, offered to color in my khaki pants with a black Sharpie. Then I laughed even harder because I was seriously considering it.

Luckily, my sister and brother-in-law pack like they're leaving the country for a month, even if they're just going around the corner, so they had an extra suit that was close enough to my size that I didn't have to show up to my father's funeral in marker-stained pants.

Anyway, how Freudian was that? This was the first time I had ever in my life been without a suit on hand, and it was the only time that it was absolutely necessary.

It was tough at the wake, because there he was, lying in front of us. The funeral was rough, too. Even though we'd waited for this moment for a long time, it was very hard once we realized he was really gone.

But the hardest time was six months later. Out of the blue, I received a check from an insurance company. Without telling anyone, many years before my father had taken out a life insurance policy with me as the sole beneficiary, and for quite a lot of money.

I had a colleague from Parsons staying with me that night. I opened the envelope, saw what he had done for me, and fell apart. We had to order takeout because I was too much of a mess to cook or go out.

He didn't do that for anyone else or tell anyone that he'd done it—not even my mother. Everyone was shocked. I told my mother that I would turn the money over to her, but she wouldn't let me.

My father and I were not close. He didn't approve of me particularly, and he was not warm and fuzzy. Maybe he was trying to make up with me? I'll never know. But it was lovely and completely unexpected. It was an act of pure generosity.

I like to think that it made him happy to make that secret gesture, and it certainly taught me a lesson about humanity. You never know what goes on inside people's heads, even when they are your flesh and blood.

That is one thing I try to keep in mind when I talk about people's behavior. I believe very strongly that we should all try our best to treat one another well, but I also know that some people who are difficult are doing their best, only their best isn't all that great. I used to be much more hard-nosed about this and about a lot of other things. But that moment when I opened up the check from my father taught me that I didn't actually know everything about him. He had things going on inside his head that I never knew and that I will probably never understand.

When someone does something cruel or rude now, I think of that.

I don't expect that in twenty years I will get a check out of the blue from the person who cuts in front of me on line at the bank. But maybe one day someone who does the same thing will realize their error and apologize. Maybe we'll all apologize for whatever we've done to hurt one another and forgive and be forgiven.

For as much as I relish being a know-it-all when it comes to fashion, when it comes to the future, I haven't got a clue. "Carry on!" is something I say to the *Project Runway* designers after I visit them in the workroom, and it's something I say to myself now: Carry on, and let's see what happens next.

❡[ACKNOWLEDGMENTS]❡

THIS BOOK WOULD NEVER have happened without the encouragement and support of a number of critical individuals. To begin, I am grateful to my agent, Jonathan Swaden of CAA, for introducing me to Peter Steinberg of the Steinberg Agency, who became my book agent. Peter has been and continues to be a boulder of support and an unflagging cheerleader. Peter helped me refine the concept of the book and, in turn, he presented a précis to several publishing houses. Patrick Price at Simon & Schuster's Gallery Books possessed such contagious enthusiasm for the book that I was instantly smitten with the imprint.

While I take great pride in authorship, Peter and Patrick understood that I would need a partner in this endeavor and, ideally, a partner who could bring to the project qualities and characteristics that I don't and won't possess. Specifically, I was looking for an individual of another gender and a younger generation. They introduced me to the divine Ada Calhoun. Without Ada, this book would have never materialized, literally. She was my conscience, my truth teller, my spiritual leader, and always a calm port. At a critical juncture, I gave Ada—and Peter and Patrick—plenty of reasons for why I felt the need to abandon the book. Those reasons were many—

too much work, too many moving parts in my life, too many competing pressures from things that I *had* to do rather than what I may *want* to do. Fortunately, these three key friends and allies were intractable and resolute. *The book must go on!* I am forever grateful to them and merely hope that we have another opportunity to work together.

Finally, I must thank my family, especially my mother (god willing, she won't read this book, because it may kill her) and sister. And I must acknowledge all the people in my life who unknowingly provided so much of the content of this book. Thank you!